KEYS

TO LIVING A

HAPPY AND REGRET-FREE LIFE

SANTOSH JOSHI

Originally published in India by:
Embassy Books
120 Great Western Building,
Maharashtra Chamber of Commerce Lane
Fort, Mumbai - 400023, India

Under the title *Keys*
By Santosh Joshi
Copyright © 2015 - Santosh Joshi - India

For more information on foreign distribution, call 717-530-2122.
Reach us on the Internet: www.soundwisdom.com.
Sound Wisdom
P.O. Box 310
Shippensburg, PA 17257-0310

ISBN 13 TP: 978-0-7684-1177-5
ISBN 13 Ebook: 978-0-7684-1178-2

For Worldwide Distribution, Printed in the U.S.A.
1 2 3 4 5 6 7 8 / 18 17

CONTENTS

Preface   7

Introduction: Our Three Selves   11

KEY #1—HEAL YOUR PAST

Chapter 1 Bygones Are Bygones?   25

Chapter 2 Rediscover the Real You   39

Chapter 3 Travel Light—Offload Emotional Residue   51

Chapter 4 Reliving Is Relieving   61

Chapter 5 Your Inner Child—the Fountain of Joy   71

Chapter 6 The Gift of Forgiveness   83

Chapter 7 Healing Your Past   95

Chapter 8 Powerful Tools to Heal Yourself   99

KEY #2—LIVE YOUR PRESENT

Chapter 1 Life's Greatest Gift—The Present Moment   111

Chapter 2 Discover Your Purpose   125

Chapter 3 Choice Is Your Birthright—Exercise It   137

Chapter 4 Just Do It—Now   153

Chapter 5 The Unstoppable You   167

Conclusion: The Next Step   181

PREFACE

When I was young, we raised some pets at home. By that I mean we had a few birds locked up in a metal cage. Whenever I went near the cage, the birds would flutter their wings with the hope that I would open the door and set them free. But, perhaps due to my young age, I didn't understand the pain and the agony these birds were going through. I was very proud of my possessions and even bragged about them incessantly.

Until one day, I found myself trapped in the enclosure of "Dos and Don'ts." What a misery it is to be shackled by chains! That day I empathized with these ill-fated birds. I didn't waste any more time; I opened the door of the cage and said to the birds, "Go...fly high! Your place is up there!" pointing my finger toward the sky. As the birds soared high in the sky, so did my heart in joy and the peace that comes with doing the right thing.

After living in a set pattern, living the life that was designed for me and not by me, one fine day I decided to break free like the birds and pursue my dream destiny—to enrich others' lives. It was a difficult call as it meant completely downsizing my life. But the hope of achieving my purpose gave me the strength needed. I stepped into an arena that was completely dark, holding the torch of faith. I set on my mission to help people heal themselves and discover their true potential.

Since then I have developed a few techniques on my own and gathered many experiences—some from my own life and some from the people who came to me for sessions—and I decided to put them all together in book form.

During my workshops, I interacted with many people and found the cause of all unhappiness and misery centered on the regrets, worries, anxieties, and insecurities of life. Rather than living the precious moments life offers, we either live in the past or the future, when the truth is the former has already gone and the latter is yet to come.

I discovered that to live the present moment, we have to heal our past and plan for our future. This book will give you the means to do so, and enable you to live a successful, fulfilling, and peaceful life.

My workshops that helped many people reflected the HLP philosophy—Heal, Live, Plan—and participants, who had come to me with issues such as unhealthy relationships, ill health, unsuccessful careers, etc., found solutions to their problems. I found that healing, living, and planning are the three most powerful KEYS to unlock the highest potential in each of us, thus paving a way to a highly successful life. These keys are freely available to all. We just need to pick them up and open the door to our dreams. It was most rewarding to see positive and radical changes in the people who came to me who implemented the HLP philosophy. This gave me immense strength to move forward on my own journey to share the keys to a wider audience, including you!

Writing this book has been a journey for me from my past to my future. Each chapter has been a chapter of my life. Each and every word have come from my heart, and I believe that whatever comes from the heart reaches the heart. I believe that we are all joint travelers on this journey and should benefit from each other and help each other grow.

I urge you to read one chapter at a time, relate to it, absorb it, digest it, and then move ahead. I have created blank spaces throughout the book titled "Thoughts" so you can write your thoughts while reading. At the end of each section, there is an interactive exercise that will help you know yourself better, followed by some powerful tools that can be used immediately. All my genuine and sincere efforts will come to fruition if what I share touches you and pushes you to change your life for the better.

During the process of writing, I have come to realize that each person is unique and deserves the best we can aim for. Each of us has the potential to reach the skies and touch many lives. If you read using your heart instead of your mind, you will be a completely changed person—a person who walks through life joyfully and fulfills your destiny by taking complete charge of your daily activities and leading a life full of happiness, contentment, and peace.

INTRODUCTION

OUR THREE SELVES

Knock-knock…

Knock-knock…

"Anybody home? Please open the door…I need to talk to you!"

The frantic knock at the door and a desperate and somewhat hysterical voice stirred me out of my deep sleep. I was slightly disoriented as I woke up, and found that my pulse was racing. I could literally hear my heart pounding in the stillness of night. I was sweating profusely. I came to my senses, as the clock struck two. Is this a nightmare? I wondered. Or is my mind simply playing games? Who wants to visit me in the middle of night?" I said to myself and got out of my bed to fetch a glass of water, dismissing my thoughts.

Knock-knock…

Knock-knock…

"Please open the door and let me in. I need you, please help me," said the pleading voice again.

That's when I realized that somebody was really at the door. The voice seemed familiar. Still, I was irritated at the stranger disturbing my peaceful sleep in the middle of the night. Reluctantly, I walked toward the main door to check on the stranger. Peeping through the eyehole, I was shocked at what I saw. In front of the door stood someone who looked just like me. Only he was younger and looked haggard. He was carrying a huge bag over his back that appeared to weigh him down. His clothes were in tatters and his shoes worn out. His childlike face was hidden behind what seemed like years of exhaustion. This sight made me nervous.

"Who are you?" I asked anxiously from the other side without opening the door.

"I am your Past Self, please open the door and let me in," came the reply, with more desperation than before.

I was puzzled with his reply. Who is this stranger who looks like me, calls himself my Past Self and asks for my help; that too at an unearthly hour! Why does this past self have to come and rob me of my calm in the middle of the night? I could feel the resistance building up. I gathered my nerve and opened the door.

In a polite yet firm voice I told Past Self, "Listen, I am sorry, but I cannot help you right now. Can you please come to-morrow afternoon? I need to get some sleep, as I have a couple of important meetings in the morning."

Without even waiting for a reply, I almost slammed the door. When I looked through the eyehole again, I saw Past Self turn away and leave, disappointed. I had lost my sleep by then and spent the rest of the night tossing and turning, thinking about this strange visitor who called himself my Past Self.

As the sun rose, spreading its warm blanket all over, I got out of my bed feeling totally drained and gloomy. I made a hot cup of ginger tea for myself and sat in my garden, sipping the tea, pondering what happened last night.

I was blessed with a beautiful garden and a huge mansion and all that any human being would long for. I was always full of exuberance, focused on my goals, and a go-getter. People were envious of me as I always appeared happy and cheerful. My mantra in life was "Live in the moment." I was truly grateful for all that I had in life.

But something changed that night, and I didn't feel the same. I felt haunted by Past Self. He had completely taken away my peace and calm. It was puzzling why the brief encounter with Past Self had frightened me so. It had stirred me deep within. Though I asked Past Self to come in the afternoon, I was not too keen to face him again.

I had to cancel the meetings planned for the morning as I was feeling low. I needed to change my state of mind. I decided to discuss this with my newfound friend, Future Self. Since Future Self and I were planning a few ventures together, I thought it would be appropriate to talk about this incident with him.

In the short acquaintance that we had, I found myself getting pulled toward Future Self due to his magnetic personality. Though he had a mysterious character, he always radiated hope. He exhibited enormous faith in his own potential and the universe. Future Self was always optimistic even in the darkest hour, and came up with positive and brilliant solutions for any problem under the sun. The only problem was that he was unpredictable most of the times. He did not behave the way I expected him to most often. Hence I was unsure if he would willingly help me.

I picked up my mobile phone and dialed my friend Future Self's number.

"Hi Present Self, I was just thinking about you. How are you my friend?" said Future Self, in his ever-enthusiastic voice. "What is it that is troubling you, my dear?" he added without waiting for my reply. I knew that my friend had good intuitive sense, which made me trust him and the advice he offered.

"I am feeling very anxious and gripped by worry and fear," I said.

"But that is not your true nature. My friend Present Self, as I know him, is always happy and full of life!"

"Yeah! You're right Future Self. But today the situation is different. Anyhow, I want to come out of this state. I want to be happy and energetic at every moment, again."

"So what's the matter?" asked Future Self.

I narrated what happened that night. Future Self lent me a patient ear. Then on a very promising note, he advised, "The best way to deal with anything that is bothering you is to face it. Go and face Past Self and see what he wants to tell you. Don't assume things. If you get worried and anxious about anything, you will lose focus in life. You need to achieve certain goals. If you are scared and run away from Past Self, he will keep haunting you. So go and face him. The choice that you make at every moment will decide where you reach in the future. So have faith and march ahead fearlessly. Listen to your heart and just do it!" said my friend Future Self.

This profound wisdom from my friend gave me a lot of strength and courage to face Past Self with renewed vigor. I said to myself, Yes! I can do it!

As expected, Past Self promptly arrived in the afternoon. I opened the door, hugged him, and gave him a warm welcome. "Welcome my friend, please come inside," I said, after apologizing for my rude behavior the previous night.

I asked him to sit on the sofa as I went to the kitchen to get some water. When I came back to the living area, I saw Past Self huddled up in the corner of the sofa, giving me a frightened look. He must have felt exceedingly startled by my changed behavior.

"Tell me, how can I help you?" I asked lovingly, offering him the glass of water. I took a seat near Past Self, held his hand, and said, "Don't be afraid. Trust me, I really mean to help you in every possible way I can."

At this point, Past Self burst out crying. I allowed him to cry his heart out. After a while, he wiped his tears with both his shoulders and hands. Still sobbing, he said, "Present Self, I am in great trouble and I seek your help. In fact, you are the only person who can help me out of this situation. I am troubled by a lot of enemies. A few of them are Remorse, Guilt, Anger, Fear, and Sorrow. They follow me everywhere and have made my life miserable. If they keep pestering me, I have no option but to end my life. I just can't deal with them. They have even threatened to attack and ruin you very soon. I am petrified. I need your help in dealing with them. You are my only hope now." And Past Self started weeping again.

"Yes, it is a grave situation," I murmured to myself.

I got up from the couch and hugged Past Self tightly, and said, "Don't worry. I am with you, and we will handle this together. Everything is going to be fine. Have faith!"

I decided to put everything else on hold and give this situation my complete attention and priority. We sat together and spent the whole evening making plans to deal with our now common enemies. I told Past Self, "The best way to deal with our enemies is to first acknowledge and accept them; and then make peace with them and let them go. The more we engage in battle, the more we will be hurt, as they are a mighty force. If we resist them they will persist. So the best deal would be to make peace with them and let them go."

Past Self agreed to my plan and we started implementing it, targeting one enemy at a time. It was not an easy task. As we tried dealing with one enemy, the others would try to dissuade us from our goal. Though it took us quite some time and a lot of effort, we finally succeeded in our endeavor. My friend Past Self was completely at peace and now there was no possibility of threat from our enemies to him or me.

Eventually, all three of us, Past Self, Future Self, and myself (Present Self), became thick friends. To celebrate the victory of our battle against our enemies, I hosted a dinner at my place. I was truly happy to see a contented smile on my friend Past Self's face. My friend Future Self was as bright as ever. His eyes were full of hope. It was a beautiful reunion of three long lost friends. We raised a toast to our friendship.

That evening, we vowed to be always present for each other, in any situation. After we finished dinner, Past Self quietly sat on the corner sofa, completely fearless and relaxed, enjoying the dessert. As I glanced at Past Self, he gave me a look filled with love and gratitude. With a satisfied smile on my face, future self and I got engrossed in planning our future. I experienced bliss like never before. This was the best day of my life, as I felt happy, peaceful, and complete.

*   *   *

It is important for the three parts of our personality—past self, present self, and future self—to be in harmony with each other. These are the three dimensions of life. Usually these three dimensions get disjoint with time because of unresolved issues of the past, or the fears, anxieties, and insecurities of the future. Living in just one dimension and ignoring the other two ultimately results in a fragmented life.

Many of us will ignore our past and think only about the present and the future; or ignore the future and spend lot of time brooding about past issues. Some people live only in the present, which is actually the best thing to do. However, their past issues are haunting them or they are too scared to think about the future. The key to a successful life is integrating these three dimensions of life into one.

Here I introduce to you the HLP principle, meaning **H**ealing the past, **L**iving in the present, and **P**lanning for the future. These are basically the three KEYS that open the gateway to a successful life—a life where all your dreams are waiting to be achieved. All three keys are important, and we need to work on each of them to achieve your best in life. This book serves as a guide to do exactly this.

To live successfully, ask yourself these three questions at every point in life:

1. Do I ever get affected by bad memories from the past and the emotions attached to them?

2. Am I happy, peaceful, and content and using my best potential in the present moment?

3. Am I often insecure and anxious about my future?

The answers to these questions will tell the extent of fragmentation of your *self*. They will tell you where you are living most of the time—in the past, present, or future. If the answer is other than the present, then it is time to seriously start work on integrating your *self*.

We are usually so complacent where we are that only when we realize that there is no escaping the situation do we step out of our comfort zone. We must understand that when we enter the *discomfort* zone from our *comfort* zone, it always leads to a larger comfort zone, and the process thus continues if we are to advance toward achieving our goals.

What happens when we hear other people's success stories? Don't we feel motivated and inspired? Don't we feel that we can do it as well? Of course we do. Why then, are most of us unable to reach where we belong—at the top?

Here is the answer. Most people are not aware of the immense potential they have within. They are like sleeping giants who have forgotten about their own powers—the power to take on the world, to achieve great success, to win. Even if they realize their massive strength, whenever they come across a difficulty or an opportunity in life, an inner dialogue with self begins. It is the dialogue between our past, present, and future selves.

Our past self will bring to the surface all the incidents in our lives when we failed miserably. It will try to convince us about our lack of abilities in accomplishing the task. Our future self will make us anxious by projecting all the fears that could be encountered if we do undertake the task. Ultimately we end up not taking up the challenge. We are so ruled by our past and future that we miss the strength and beauty of our present, which is the only reality, the only truth.

We live life floating like a raft in an ocean getting swayed by the waves in all possible directions. But deep within, we all have the burning desire to take complete charge of our lives. Only when we kindle this desire and take charge of our life can we actually sail toward our goals. *The choice lies with us.* This book is the first step in committing yourself to becoming who you want to see in yourself.

KEY #1

HEAL YOUR PAST

DO WE REALLY?

Do we really forget what we've been through?
Or do we remember all, just pretend not to?
When we say "I moved on," do we really mean it?
Or just convince ourselves, not meaning one bit.

Bygones are never really bygones, my dear friend.
We just try to forget the past, never realizing an end.
Past is important, as it teaches us lessons
And gives us insights, much valuable ones;

But hurts of the past, we all need to heal
Offloading residual emotions, we so badly feel.
It's good to heal memories and agonies of the past,
As they slow our progress, as long as they last.

We are like onions, with many layers of conditioning;
Our real self is the center, to which these layers cling.
Conditioning pulls us back from our highest goal
And makes us forget the purpose of our soul.

We can heal emotions, memories with painful feeling
By revisiting the past, as reliving is relieving.
Forgiveness is a great tool to relieve us of baggage
That we have been carrying since a tender age.

Each one of us inside has a tiny little child
Who craves for attention, and is ready to go wild.
It just needs our love and a little pampering,
Living, that little child makes us happy beings.

So let's heal our past and move ahead to achieve
And make traveling light our motto to live.

CHAPTER 1

BYGONES ARE BYGONES?

I thought it is forgotten, but my past was always there
Unknowingly following me, hiding from the glare.
It is good for me to recognize this fact;
It helps me in, putting together my act.

As I walked through the valley, I knew I was not alone. Even though it was quiet, I felt something follow me. I feared its presence and hurried through the valley gasping for breath. My journey was uncomfortable and miserable. The more I tried to run away from it, the more it chased me. But I was too afraid to turn back, so I continued hastily in fear.

When I reached halfway through the valley, I got tired and was angry at myself for being afraid. So I took a moment, gathered courage and said to myself, *If I have to go any farther, I'm going to do it fearlessly; I will not take one more step until I have conquered this fear.* Curious about what I would find, I gathered all my strength and turned back right that moment. I was astonished at what I saw.

It was my own shadow, nothing else! It had been following me quietly, creating fear and doubt and slowing my pace. I had nothing to fear as it was only a reflection of me; and when I realized that, I was no longer afraid. Then I walked ahead fearless and triumphant.

Identifying the cause of our fears of the past is what rids us of them and makes our journey better.

*   *   *

Just relax. It's been a long time. No one will remember you, don't look so troubled, and cheer up, I reassured myself by repeating these words to suppress the guilt I felt deep within. I was equally excited and nervous about visiting my old school after twenty long years.

As I slowly walked through the main gate into the school, where I spent a wonderful decade of my life, I reflected on how amazing and carefree those days were. I looked around and saw that not much had changed. Children were racing around each other in the playground. Teachers walked through the grounds, serene and focused. My school was as vibrant as ever.

When I approached the principal's office, my heart was racing. I knew exactly what was bothering me, but tried to hide it with a broad smile, fearing someone might just figure it all out. The principal was friendly, and in a while, I inquired about the former principal and teachers of my yonder years. I learned that most of them had retired, but my physics teacher was still teaching a class at the school. The current principal insisted that I meet with him. Reluctantly, not knowing a polite way to ignore his enthusiastic offer, I agreed.

As I walked to the staff room, my pulse started racing again, the color from my face drained. Pale and breathless, I entered the staff room with the principal. There he was, my physics teacher, seated at the far end of a table, near a window, quietly reading a book. I walked up to him and introduced myself. He recognized me right away and smiled as he gave me a big hug. He said he was very proud of me as he knew I was doing well in life.

I thanked him for the compliment and said, "That is because of your guidance and blessings, sir. You know I wasn't good at physics."

My teacher replied with a smile, "It was my duty to teach you and your duty to learn, and I believe we both did our duties well!"

I thanked him, and after spending a few minutes, I left the staff room. I sat on a bench near the playground and suddenly my eyes were filled with tears; tears of guilt and remorse, tears of anger at myself for what a bunch of friends and I had done to this teacher when we were in our final year of school.

My whole group was excited to leave school and enter college. It felt like we were finally going to taste real freedom. Freedom from wearing uniforms, freedom from being constantly reprimanded by teachers, freedom from being on time, doing homework, and all the things that school-life demands. Our lives were about to change and a whole new world awaited us outside the walls of this school. Surely a bit of mischief was not really going to hurt anyone, right?

And so we decided to play a prank. We had a group meeting to choose our target and what would be his ill fate. The next day was the last day of classes before exams began and the last class was physics. It was a hot summer day and as soon as our teacher walked in, he switched on the fan and sat down to wipe off his sweat.

Suddenly something fell from above and landed on the teacher's head. We, the conspirators, screamed loudly, "Snake! Snake! Run, it's a snake!"

The poor teacher ran toward the corridor and screamed, "Get it off! Get it off my head!"

All of us ran after him to see how it would end. The teacher was looking down the ledge with dismay and despair. And when we looked at him, we were shocked out of our wits. Our poor physics teacher was bald. What we had thought to be a thick matt of black silky hair was actually a wig.

The wig that was the saving grace of a young man had fallen three stories down, along with the rubber snake, which we had planted on top of the ceiling fan. The kids started laughing at the sight of this, which left him completely embarrassed. He came into the class, collected his books and left.

Alarm bells started ringing in our ears at the thought of what would happen if anyone found out we had done it. We could smell danger in the air as we looked at each other silently with guilty eyes. Later that day, we vowed not to say a word about it to anyone.

Contrary to what we suspected, nothing happened. The exams were finished, and on the last day of school was our farewell party. The principal addressed the entire class. He began by thanking the teachers and congratulating the batch of students for completing their years at the school. He said, "I'm very happy for all of you. As you leave, I wish you all the best for your further studies and hope that you will make us and your parents proud."

Then he added, "I wish to take this opportunity to inform you all that a recent mischief has been reported to me. I even know the names of the mischief-makers, but I want to give them a second chance in the hope that they will change. Remember that when you leave a place, as you are doing today, leave with pride and good memories. Make sure that people remember you for the right reasons. It is very difficult to build a good reputation as it takes a long time; however, it just takes a couple of seconds to spoil it. So always choose your words and actions carefully. I hope the students responsible for this mischief reflect on what they have done and how it has hurt the person who suffered embarrassment for no mistake of his."

The principal then continued his speech, talking about other things, but by then I was deaf with guilt. This incident took place years ago, yet as I sat on the bench, I vividly recollected everything. How is it that I was still so guilty about something that had happened years ago? How can this feeling be powerful even today?

One thing was very clear though, I was still harboring the guilt of that mischief, but most of the time pretended that it didn't exist. So then I questioned myself, *Am I still guilty of what I had once happily participated in? Is it possible that what we think of as old forgotten memories are actually skeletons in the closet, waiting to fall out at the very first chance? Are we then lying to ourselves? Are bygones really bygones, or are we living a myth?*

THOUGHTS

_____

_____

_____

THE PAST REMAINS

All our lives are similar in a way. On one hand we assure ourselves that everything is forgotten, that bygones are bygones; and on the other hand we walk through life worrying about the shadows of our past. These shadows follow us quietly and shock us when we notice them, which happens from time to time. Sometimes we are aware of their presence, but most of the time we fail to understand or recognize them. In fact, we can never really let go of these shadows completely.

When camping in the forest, we usually light a bonfire. However, before leaving the campsite, we cover it up with mud to put out the fire. What we don't realize is although on the surface the fire has been put out, it is still alive and burning underneath. And if not put out completely and quickly, there is a risk of the small bonfire burning through the entire forest. Similarly, certain incidents from our past, which seem small and insignificant and we feel they can be ignored, can grow to become disasters. Ignoring something will not make it go away; rather, it will surface in our thoughts again and again, causing repeated pain and anguish. And each time it resurfaces, the pain increases manifold.

The first thing to do is to accept the real possibility of an issue causing us unhappiness. Then, identify the cause of that issue or issues—an event, person, place, when it happened, and the dominating emotion behind that feeling. This step is vital in the process of healing. We humans operate only from two kinds of emotions:

Love-based emotions (happiness, compassion, courage, and kindness) or
Fear-based emotions (anger, hatred, resentment, and regret)

All our life activities are initiated by love or fear. When we are operating from a love-based emotion, we are happy. It is when we operate from a fear-based emotion that we feel disturbed and bothered. And it is surprising how easily we get disturbed by something that happened in the past.

Most of us will be able to precisely recall a particular incident from the past, the pain it caused and the time it happened.

The fact that we can remember a particular incident so vividly clearly indicates how the whole incident is still embedded in our minds. That is the marvel of the human mind, it recollects everything.

Because every incident that occurs in our lives is recorded and carefully stored away in our minds as memories, they then become part of our past. The mind is not biased when recording a memory; it does not discriminate between negative or positive, good or bad. Its job is to record and store. Therefore we are able to recall most events quickly and accurately, the good and the bad ones alike.

But the past is not to be disowned, as there is much to be cherished from it. Whatever we are today is a result of the past—upbringing, conditioning, teachings, experiences, memories, and relationships. In reality, nothing is good or bad (as we may label them), it's just the perception we hold. Every event is a result of the choices we make at any point in our lives and follow it up with a corresponding action. But some things are beyond our understanding, such as an accidental death, for example.

However, there are no coincidences in life, and nothing is accidental. Everything in our lives happened or is happening for a reason. It may not seem so during that time, but in hindsight we will realize that reason. What we need to focus on, however, are the emotions from the past that show up from time to time, causing pain and disturbance in our present. These emotions need to be identified and addressed, as they are the ones that cause havoc in our lives.

I come across so many people who try to convince me that their past is of no significance to them. They claim to have forgotten the unhappy and hurtful events from the past, that they no longer bother them and that they have forgiven everyone who hurt them. They say they love living in the present, at all times. I wish they knew how far from the truth this confession is.

One of the biggest myths of our lives is bygones are bygones. Bygones literally mean something gone by, in the past, no longer in the present. Every time we use the phrase "bygones are bygones," we need to question ourselves and honestly answer if it holds true to the event or situation we use it for.

Have we really forgotten, completely let go of the pain and hurt caused by something that happened in the past? Or are we just not aware of its presence in our lives? Or is it that we are aware but are trying to deny the existence of that painful past, which is very much there?

How can we be sure or validate that we are still holding on to the negative emotions from the past? A simple way to validate that bygones are *not* bygones is to relate your emotions to a particular place, event, or person and see how you feel. Think about suddenly bumping into a person whom you have not seen for a long time. What would your reaction be when suddenly coming face to face with the person? What emotions would you relate to that chance encounter? Do you feel happy, sad, or absolutely nothing?

The emotions that you feel at that exact moment on seeing that person will depend on the experiences you shared in the past. If you have had a bad experience, a flood of emotions such as anger, pain, and misery will come gushing out of you. This is enough to validate that bygones are not bygones.

A CHANCE ENCOUNTER

To illustrate my point, let me share another personal incident. Few years after I had left one of my first corporate jobs, I was trying to set-up my own business. I met a friend at a coffee shop to discuss a business proposal. On my way back home, I stopped at a music store to pick up a few CDs. As I was going through the rack of new arrivals, I suddenly came face to face with my archrival at that time.

I stood just inches away from a man who had caused me much agony in the past. He was the one who had very meticulously planned to blame me for something I had not done. I was being held responsible for something that was completely against my principles and work ethics. He knew I was innocent, but had some grudge against me. He was instrumental in my ouster from the job. In a matter of seconds, everything from that past flashed before my eyes. I was filled with so much anger and rage that I could have punched his face right there.

When he finally noticed me, he was speechless. We exchanged awkward smiles and he left hastily. After a while, I left the store, with the CDs tightly clutched in my hands. As I walked home, I remembered everything this man had done to hurt and embarrass me. I was filled with immense pain and felt extremely angry at myself for not having said anything to him when all this actually happened, or when I saw him at the music store.

At home I sat quietly on the couch for a long time. When my wife noticed me sitting in an unnaturally stiff way, she asked me what was wrong. I told her about the whole incident and how angry I was on seeing him. My wife understood my pain, as she knew what I had been put through by that guy. She asked me to cheer up and said, "Listen, it's been five years now. Isn't it time you moved on? Don't allow him to get to you like this…we live in the same city and you might bump into him again. Do you want to relive this pain again and again? Bygones are bygones, let it be."

For a long time, I thought about what my wife had said and asked myself a series of questions. It is one of the things I do when I come across a problem. I write down a series of questions and answer them to find solutions to the problem on hand. I asked myself: *What would I do if I came across him again, would I react in the same way? Would I be as angry as I was today or would the anger lessen with time? Do the painful memories of the past reduce in intensity with passing time? Or do they just get suppressed until they are unleashed by a reminder of that incident and rise like a deadly serpent, ready to attack?*

Easier said than applied, bygones are *not* bygones, and the sooner we realize this the easier it becomes for us to find a solution. Ignoring the problem is like sweeping dirt under the carpet. This only hides the dust where we cannot see it. *But the dirt is still there, and we are always aware of that truth.*

When the base of a wooden house is infested with termites, it has to be properly treated at the base; otherwise there is a risk that the entire house will eventually collapse. Similarly, there are no quick fixes to get rid of the heavy load of negative emotions that we carry in life. We have to take the necessary measures to rectify the situation. The longer we ignore a problem, the worse it will become.

Bygones are never really bygones, because everything that has happened in the past has an effect on who, what, and where we are today. Everything we do today will have an impact on us tomorrow. What may seem good now may not be so a few months later. Also, what may seem bad now may not be so either. It is important to revisit the past and learn the lessons from all that has happened. We must analyze how it plays a role in shaping our decisions, our thoughts, and our actions in the present.

The heavy burden of fear-based emotions that we carry from our past triggers many of the unhappy and unpleasant situations in our present. These suppressed emotions act as road blocks that slow our progress in life. There are many who live with a lot of guilt, not aware of the cause of their misery and pain. They should understand that it's easier to let go and move on once they acknowledge that the past is still affecting their present and try to understand what needs to be addressed.

Unless we acknowledge the past, and until we learn the lessons, it will keep repeating itself—over and over again. The repetitive events in our life signal us toward an underlying problem, cautioning us to become aware. All we have to do is identify the pattern and work on it.

The ultimate question you must ask yourself: *How do I want to live my life…in the bygone-lane or in the present-lane?* If the answer is the latter, acknowledge and realize that you are consciously carrying the negative emotions of your traumatic past. That you are still holding on to them and these are truly the blocking stones on your path to being a happier, healthier, and successful individual.

This is the first step toward healing yourself of the past. Once you have this realization, the journey of transformation begins; turning you into your best, brilliant self.

Now that the realization has set in, that bygones are not bygones, what next?

AT A GLANCE

• The past remains in your mind, even if you tend to forget it.

• Past emotions, hurts, anger, guilt, and resentments pull you back from becoming all you can be.

• It is important to acknowledge issues in the past that evoke emotions.

• You can learn much from your past.

CHAPTER 2

REDISCOVER THE REAL YOU

"Who am I?" When I asked myself, I heard a feeble voice.
To understand its message, I had to silent outer noise.
I realized it is coming from deep within my heart.
My self lies under layers that I need to tear apart.

WE ARE LIKE ONIONS

When I thought of writing this book, I needed solitude. I needed to go to a place where I could be at peace with myself and write. A friend offered his cottage, somewhere in the outskirts of the city, in the forest.

What more could I ask for? This seemed like the perfect place. He informed me that it had not been used for a very long time and thus required minor repairs and cleaning. I told him how grateful I was of his gift and agreed to take care of the repairs. My wife was equally excited about me staying at the cottage.

The next day, I packed my bags and drove out. When I reached the quaint town, I was greeted by the caretaker of the cottage. With a big smile, he introduced himself as Khinchu. He said that it would take another fifteen minutes to reach the cottage and his home was close by.

As we drove, I noticed how scenic the place was and thought to myself, *Wow! This is the perfect place for me to write.* The place was breathtakingly beautiful; surrounded by tall trees, wild flowers, and a stream flowing so gently that I could barely hear it. Then the cottage came into view and my first reaction was, "Oh my heavens! This *can't* be it!" I looked at Khinchu and he smiled gaily.

When I went inside, I saw that the place was totally rundown and needed *major* repairs and cleaning. Although my mind asked me to turn around and go back, the surroundings had played their magic on my heart and I decided to stay. I immediately called my wife, who is an interior designer, and described to her what was before me. She jumped wholeheartedly into the chore, gave me some tips on how to go about restoring it, and made a list of all the things I had to buy.

Now, I got really energized; it was just like I was back in school and doing a project. I went back to town and picked up all the things on the list. That night I was Khinchu's guest. The next day when we began work on the cottage, I realized this wasn't going to be the fun project I had imagined it to be. Khinchu had asked a friend to help us who agreed to, bless his heart.

It took the three of us three days to remove all the junk from the house. It cost us a cut on my leg, bruises on our hands, and bodies as stiff as logs, but we were successful. We were able to scrape off old paint from the walls and remove the old wooden flooring.

At the end of the third day, when I sat outside sipping a cup of local *masala chai*, my thoughts went to how similar our lives are to my current situation. We are like the old cottage, conditioned to a certain way of life. As we grow older, we create belief systems of our own and sit cozily ensconced, locked up in the dense forest. Years of neglect and layers of dirt and moisture forms the fungus of conditioning. And eventually we start to rot.

It is only with great difficulty and through sheer determination that we can take up the task to restore and renew ourselves. It may be difficult, it may be painful, or we may get hurt and bruised in the process, but it *has* to be done. Living with unhealthy or unwise conditioning or belief systems is like putting fresh paint on rotting walls. The paint will chip off in no time.

The next few days were filled with excitement. We began work on the walls, the plumbing, and the wooden floors. We installed new windows and doors. We were humming, making jokes, and bonding with each other, the way hard work bonds dedicated humans. It was an incredible experience.

When the cottage was restored completely, I thanked Khinchu and his friend for their help, support, and enjoyable company. I could not believe that this was the same place I almost turned away from! It was the first time I had renovated any-thing, and I felt completely rejuvenated and proud of myself. Sitting in front of the cottage, I felt a sense of peace and calm that cannot be described but only felt.

Similarly, when you remove the layers of wrong conditioning and get *in touch* with your *true self,* you will feel completely rejuvenated and refreshed.

THOUGHTS

_____

_____

_____

WHO ARE YOU?

Whenever I ask people this simple question, "Who are you?" they always start by mentioning their names, their physical attributes, what they do, their job profile and education. When I disagree by moving my head sideways, they go on to describe their emotional state, qualities, talents, abilities, likes and dislikes. The truth is, we are none of these. A person's true self is deeper and more profound than all these answers to my question.

Have you ever peeled an onion? What do you observe as you continue to peel? You have to take off layer after layer before you reach the center, the core of the onion! Have you tasted just this core of the onion? If you have, you will know that it tastes very different from the outer layers. It is actually very sweet.

We are all like that sweet core of the onion when we are born. If you notice the face of a newborn baby, you will see a glow, a sparkle, and a magical kind of calm that surrounds the baby. This in turn fills us with joy, love, and peace. Have you ever wondered what happened to the baby within you? Where did the glow disappear? What distinguished that sparkle?

Where is the *real you,* that embodiment of love and peace? The answer is simple; the real you is buried under numerous layers of conditioning.

Over the years, these layers changed us from who we originally were to someone we no longer relate to. And it is time *now* to refurbish ourselves by removing the deposits of negative beliefs that are no longer required, wanted, or needed.

The layers of onion signify the layers of beliefs that we have been covered with since the time of our birth. The first belief systems are passed on to us by our parents in the form of dos and don'ts, right and wrong, good and bad. Have you observed a baby when starting to crawl and grab things? The child experiences joy that radiates from his or her face. However, when the mother senses any trouble, she immediately stops the child, thereby stopping its natural instinct.

For instance, when the child is crawling toward the edge of the stairs, the mother (or any concerned adult) runs and grabs the child, preventing the little one from falling down the stairs— or through her expressions and words tells the child not to go ahead. When we are young, our parents tell us many such things that become imbedded in our minds. To name only a few, *Don't run too fast, you will fall down* and *Don't laugh too loudly, it's bad manners*, and so on.

The second set of conditioning starts in school. When we go to school, our teachers give us a set of rules and regulations to follow. Don't speak loudly, don't play in the mud, don't pluck flowers, don't write on the walls, etc. Then as we grow, we hear opinions about ourselves from others such as, "You are dark, you are fair, you are smart, you are dumb, you are good, you are naughty, you behave badly, you are well-behaved." The list is endless.

Those are the early days of "conditioning of the mind." The belief system that we build slowly distances us from our true self. Layer after layer keeps adding up and we don't even realize it is happening. Each layer becomes part of our lives; we identify ourselves with these belief systems and hold them to be true.

I remember when as a child I was told, "You are not supposed to cry. You are a boy." Many people I know are conditioned to believe that if they get out of bed on the wrong side or if they look at their face in the mirror first thing in the morning, their day will be ruined or something will surely go wrong. Really, how can there even be a "wrong side" of the bed and how could looking at your beautiful face decide the fate of the events that occur during the day? These are silly beliefs picked up while growing up. But because people believe them, they manifest.

The number of belief systems we continue to form throughout our lives is huge. These systems create a comfortable environment for us to thrive in; hence, making it difficult to break out of at a later age. They also seem to rule our day-to-day behavior pattern.

THE TINY CHAIN

You have probably seen an elephant at the circus. You may have noticed the tiny chain by which it is tied to a pillar after the show is over. It looks so serene and comfortable in its confinement. Have you ever wondered why a huge elephant, weighing more than 1,000 kilograms (more than 1 ton) and has the strength to carry heavy loads, does not break the tiny chain and run away? It definitely can! Any day. But the elephant is conditioned to think that it cannot.

How is this conditioning achieved? When the elephant is a baby, it is tied by the same tiny little chain, which it cannot break, even though it tries. After some time, it stops trying because it starts believing that it cannot break the chain. So even after the elephant grows up and gains enormous strength, it doesn't try to break free.

We are also conditioned to believe in certain things from the time we were born. We start believing what we are capable of and what not. This is because we have been hearing people tell us what we can and cannot do. We believe everything to be true, and rarely try to experiment or take steps to change those views. Many of us spend our entire lives in such beliefs and never explore the storehouse of potential with which we are born. Think of how you were as a child, and recall all the wonderful things that you did without any fear or inhibition. Are you still doing any of those things? If not, ask yourself why?

Various studies have shown that until the age of seven, our brains are in a dream-like state and the mind is absorbing everything from its surroundings, with no filters to differentiate anything. It's all information that we record and store without processing. But as we grow, we start putting them in different categories, like good, bad, right, wrong, pretty, ugly, tall, short, and so on. Our subconscious mind accepts and stores what we consciously believe. It does not discriminate between good or bad, positive or negative, it absorbs everything that we feed it with, consciously.

And so, if we have consciously convinced ourselves that we will fail, our subconscious mind will act upon that belief and yield according to our belief patterns. Our subconscious mind is a storehouse of memories, emotions, and belief systems. It soaks up everything like a sponge, without discrimination. Hence if a negative belief system is adopted, it will be securely stored away in our subconscious mind.

To be successful and find our true self, we have to get rid of limiting beliefs and accept new and empowering truths, such as "The future does not equal the past." If you have failed before, don't worry. Stand up and try again. Failing once doesn't mean that you are going to fail all the time. Understand that this belief system is a conditioning that has taken place over a period of time.

What we have to work on is to shed, to peel off the layers of beliefs that are limiting us from being our true self. It may be difficult and may result in pain, but if we want to reach the core, our true self, the layers have to be peeled away. No matter how painful, wrongful and unhealthy conditioning has to be shed.

THE CLAY BUDDHA

In 1954, a new temple was built in Bangkok and a large Buddha statue made of clay was brought from another town. While the statue was being lifted by a crane, it slipped, fell on mud, and developed a crack. The legend says a temple monk had a dream the same night that the statue was divinely inspired. So the next day he visited the site.

While inspecting the crack, he noticed something glittering inside. He realized that there was something more to the statue than what was perceived and told the people around. They then carefully removed layers of plaster and clay to find a beautiful pure gold Buddha statue inside.

Apparently this golden Buddha statue was covered with clay and plaster when the Burmese had threatened to attack the city. The disguise was so convincing that no one ever suspected that there was something else inside. And for a long time, while it was still covered with plaster, it was thought to be worth very little. Today, the Golden Buddha statue is seen at Wat Traimit temple, which is one of Bangkok's must-see attractions.

Our true self is exactly like the golden Buddha hidden inside the layers of conditioning. Only when we are courageous enough to shed the layers will we find our "golden self" hidden inside.

LISA AND HER MOTHER

Beliefs are created when we assign meaning to events. Many of the meanings we assign to the events of our lives are not based on truth. Lisa was always told by her mother to be silent and quiet. Over the years, Lisa started believing that she is unworthy of being listened to. However, the truth was that Lisa's mom had so much noise and residual pandemonium inside her that all additional noise annoyed her. Instead of realizing that, Lisa became a victim.

Many limiting beliefs are based on our (often child-minded) subjective, erroneous interpretation of others' actions and events. If someone we didn't know or care about committed a wrong act, we would have assigned a very different meaning to it. Or ignored it completely. If a random woman asked Lisa to be quiet, she would have probably turned a deaf ear to it. Nothing is inherently meaningful; and what others do is dictated by *their* beliefs, *their* stories.

We are the ones who assign meaning to our experiences, and from that meaning we create everything we believe about ourselves. If this truth is accepted, we can begin to take control of our beliefs. We can then change our entire lives for the better.

AT A GLANCE

- Your true self is covered with layers of conditioning.

- What you are today is the result of your past.

- Your conditioning, belief systems, form a major part of your personality

- Once you understand the layers, you can peel them off.

- Only then can you realize your true potential.

CHAPTER 3

TRAVEL LIGHT—OFFLOAD EMOTIONAL RESIDUE

My own heavy baggage, dragging me from behind,
As if I am walking on a path steep and inclined.
I slow down on my journey to my chosen goal,
My own past emotions, now taking their toll.

One afternoon while working on the PC, I noticed that it was taking too long for a file to open. At first I didn't understand what the problem was. As I closed the file, I realized that my desktop was filled with files that had been there for a very long time. I had not taken the time to clear them. It suddenly struck me that I had not serviced my laptop; and to make matters worse, the antivirus program had expired!

After a nice cup of tea, I straight away got to work. I slowly and painstakingly had to open and check each and every file. Most of the files were unnecessary and many were even infected with viruses. I didn't waste any time in deleting them. There were a few important files that I saved elsewhere. In just twenty minutes, my desktop was clean and this time the file opened within seconds.

I'm glad I took time that afternoon to clear my desktop. Had I left it unattended, there was a possibility that with so many viruses, my laptop would have eventually crashed. I would have also lost most of the important data—critical information for my workshops and seminars. Immediately I called a computer engineer and asked him to service the laptop and update the antivirus software.

It is possible that many times we download "viruses" into our lives and harbor them, completely unaware. Many people carry unwanted emotions over the years that can prove to be detrimental. It is important to identify those emotions and get rid of them as quickly as possible. When we don't take time to clear out the unnecessary emotions and excess baggage from our lives, it slows us down as well. If we don't keep a check and delete what is unwanted and dangerous, then we are surely headed toward a crash!

HEAVY BACKPACK

During a trek, I noticed my friend, Karan, carrying a huge backpack. So I teasingly asked him, "Are you setting up a home in the mountains?"

Karan replied, "Oh trust me, I'm carrying all the essentials, and you will see how helpful they are when we reach the top."

After trekking for about twenty minutes uphill, Karan started panting and sweating profusely. At one point, he was unable to progress at all. So the rest of us had to take turns carrying the "essential things" in his backpack.

About mid-day we reached the spot where we were to camp for the day. When we looked around, we were speechless by the scenic beauty of the surroundings. The place was filled with wild flowers and fruit bushes, and there was a beautiful waterfall that made the atmosphere serene. We quickly dropped our backpacks and went for a dip in the pond under the waterfall. After that, we sat in a circle and meditated.

After our time of meditation, we went about plucking and munching on the delicious fruits, under the expert guidance of a friend. We were having so much fun that we totally forgot to unpack. Meanwhile, Karan was quite grumpy. He was removing things from his backpack in a fury, when I went over and asked, "Karan, what are you doing?"

Karan replied, "What a waste of my precious energy, I carried all these things, and we haven't used any of them. I wish I had packed light; I would have enjoyed the trek much more."

I said, "Well, it's never too late. Get rid of the unwanted stuff right now, the remaining trek will be easier."

Karan was not willing to do that. But soon enough he realized it was really not worth carrying the heavy load farther. So finally he discarded all the unnecessary items. Once he gave away most of the things, his backpack was nearly empty and while climbing down, Karan had great fun and was always ahead of the group.

We all carry such unnecessary baggage in the form of residual emotions. These come from our past experiences, which have affected us deeply and have made a visible impact on our psyche. And most of the time, they show up in the form of hurt, anger, resentment, guilt, and fear. Whenever we go through an experience where we have felt one or more of these negative emotions, they are etched into our memory and travel with us at every moment.

During life's journey, when we carry excess baggage, materialistic or emotional, we are uncomfortable and unhappy. These emotions do not leave us easily; no matter how much we try. They have an immense impact on the way we behave or take decisions in the present moment. As a result, they also adversely affect our physical, mental, and emotional health. It's a great idea to shed the baggage, similar to what Karan did in the trek. However, this has to be a continuous process as we store new emotions in our minds at every moment.

So how do we manage to carry these residual emotions for so many years? Here is the answer. When an incident occurs, the feelings pertaining to that incident get recorded deep in our subconscious mind along with the memory. Just imagine there is a video recorder automatically recording each and every moment of our lives, and at the press of a button we can watch any episode. It is similar with the memories that we hold deep in our subconscious mind. They resurface each time an emotional button is pressed.

The trigger can be in the form of 1) a similar experience, 2) revisiting the same place, 3) speaking on the phone with or meeting the person involved, or 4) reading a book, seeing something in a movie or on TV, which relates even remotely to the original incident. In a nutshell, anything that reminds us of those feelings can act like a trigger. It is neither wise nor healthy to live with so much emotional baggage.

On social networking sites, you may often come across people with whom you never shared a good rapport with in the past. You may not feel like connecting with him or her. Well, that's absolutely fine, you are entirely free to choose who to "friend" with! Now pause for a moment, and recollect how this person's appearance on your mind-screen made you feel. At this point, ask an honest question, "Am I still carrying some residual emotions about this person?" In your answer lies the first step—identification. This will help you understand what you need to offload or let go from your life.

THOUGHTS

_____

_____

_____

ROOT CAUSE OF ILLNESS

It is astonishing to know how the unresolved issues and emotional residues can manifest in our physical body in the form of diseases.

Sometime back, my wife had developed a sore throat. As would be a normal course of action, she went to the doctor and got a five-day course of antibiotics. However, after the five days, she was suffering and could barely speak. She even tried all the home remedies yet saw no improvement.

Incidentally, a few weeks before the sore throat, she had a misunderstanding with a close friend. She wanted to convey her wounded feelings to this friend, but didn't get a chance. This had been bothering her ever since. Still suffering from the sore throat, my wife decided to confront her friend. She called her, clarified the misunderstanding, and resolved the issue. As soon as she finished doing this, she felt as if a heavy load had been lifted from her heart. The very next morning when she woke up, she was surprised to find that her throat was almost healed. She then realized that the underlying problem behind the sore throat was the emotion related to the misunderstanding with her friend. The moment she resolved the issue and let go of the excess emotional baggage, her throat started to heal.

Many modern-day diseases such as diabetes, high blood pressure, heart-related ailments, skin disorders, sprout from the unresolved residual emotions that we carry. Unfortunately, we have been carrying them for so long that we don't even realize they exist and they become an integral part of our personality.

Residual emotions that we suppress always show up from time to time in our daily lives until we completely offload them from the subconscious level of our mind. For this, all we need to do is identify them and get rid of them.

ONLY YOU CAN HELP YOURSELF

One evening, on the insistence of his wife, Kabir took her for a drive. Unfortunately, they met with a serious accident. Although his wife escaped with minor injuries, Kabir had to undergo leg surgery. The doctors saved his leg but informed him that he would face difficulty walking throughout his life. Kabir was passionate about trekking, and this accident totally shattered him.

Today, petty things annoy Kabir and he ends up arguing with his wife at the drop of a hat. He couldn't understand why and how he could get angry so quickly at his wife, when in fact, he loves her dearly. The truth is, Kabir holds his wife responsible for his state today, and the arguments are a result of the residual emotions he is harboring deep in his subconscious mind. The emotions are being vented as angry arguments with his wife.

In a similar case, Mandira continues to harbor a lot of fear and doubt about the men she dates. She is extremely cautious, defensive, and never trusts anyone completely. This is the result of a bad breakup she went through after an eight-year relationship. She did everything in her capacity to save the relationship. However, it eventually came to a point where she had to give up, and they parted ways. The mistrust, fear, and insecurity that she displays in her current relationships come from the emotions related to that breakup. The emotions she is carrying, unaware, are ruining her chance to a happy life in the present.

Both Kabir and Mandira are destroying their present because of emotions from the past that may have no connection with them in the present. We are often so comfortable in that space of feeling victimized that we don't want to come out of it willingly.

Kabir's wife understands the real reason behind these arguments so she ignores them and makes every effort to keep him happy. Mandira's partner has moved on and has no clue of what she is going through. We need to understand that we, ourselves, are ruining our chances of being happy by thinking about something that has long gone. We need to ask ourselves: Is it worth it? Have we gained anything? Are we satisfied with the outcome? If not, then we must let it go. Remember that it is not only our present that stands the risk of being affected but we are very likely to mess up our future too.

Therefore, please pause and ask yourself, *What is it that bothers me? When am I finally going to give up this baggage? How much more of my precious present and future life am I willing to sacrifice for the past?*

It is most important to first *identify and acknowledge* the enormous collection of residual emotions that we are unknowingly carrying, and which are seriously harmful for our present and future. The next step is to *clean or clear* these emotions from our system. By doing so, we are giving ourselves a second chance to make a new beginning, to be happy, to be complete, to fulfill our dreams and desires, and to be at peace.

AT A GLANCE

• Everyone carries baggage of residual emotions from the past, even you.

• You must acknowledge and get rid of residual emotions.

• Residual, harmful emotions are the root cause of most of your illnesses.

• Only you can help yourself.

CHAPTER 4

RELIVING IS RELIEVING

My past is very much still part of what I am;
My memories, emotions—even if I don't give a damn.
I can revisit my past whenever I wish to,
To know myself better and it helps me heal too.

REVISING PAST MEMORIES

As a child, I was terrified of the dark and could not stand being in the dark for even a moment. In the dark lived the monsters who would, I thought, crop up, grab me with their gigantic claws, and eat me up.

After I grew up, I had forgotten all about my fear of the dark until one day something made me realize that I still harbored that fear. I decided to overcome this fear by reliving it. As I sat in the dark room, I finally faced my childhood fears head-on.

I recalled all the gruesome stories that frightened me and realized that it was only a creation of my mind.

When I had relived my fears I was relieved, and even though I was still sitting in the dark, I was no longer scared.

*   *   *

On my birthday a few years ago, I received a parcel from an old school friend. I quickly opened it and found a photo album and on the cover I read, "All the wonderful memories captured here." When I opened the album, the first picture was of my classmates and me. Some friends from school had put together an album of old pictures from school functions, picnics, birthday parties, and all the other times we had spent together as kids.

What a fantastic gift! Everyone at home suddenly got very excited to see the album. As we gathered around to look at the photographs, the old memories came alive. Each photograph had a unique story. I could precisely remember the details and also recall when it was taken. I had so much fun that day; and just by going through the old photographs, I virtually went back to those moments.

It is amazing how powerful our minds are and what it is capable of. Just by going through an album, I could remember so accurately the incidents and events from my school days. It almost felt like I was reliving those days.

It is indeed a pleasant trip, walking through memory lane and reminiscing about the "good old days." The pertinent question, however, is what if we were presented an album of the bad memories? How many of us are willing to look at an album filled with all the traumatic, unhappy, and bad photographs from our past? How many of us are willing to relive an *unpleasant* past?

Many people would avoid going to that lane and even reassure themselves and others alike that it is completely unnecessary and a waste of time. They see no point in remembering a past that has caused hurt and pain. As mentioned before, our minds are not selective when storing the incidents of our lives; it stores anything and everything that we experience. Therefore, just as we are able to remember all the good old days, filled with pleasant and happy experiences, we also remember the bad and unpleasant ones, from time to time. Yet, we try very hard to pretend to have forgotten them and console ourselves that they no longer bother us.

Our minds are powerhouses that store all our experiences as memories, and is divided into two parts—the conscious and the subconscious. The subconscious mind comprises about 96 percent of the mind, while the conscious mind only about 4 percent. This is most often compared to an iceberg floating in water, where only the tip is visible above. The vast portion that is under water is what our subconscious mind is like; while the conscious mind is like the tip of the iceberg that is above water.

The subconscious mind is similar to a huge safety deposit box in which are hidden all the knowledge, experiences, and all our hidden potential. Everything we have experienced from our past is safely stored in the subconscious mind in the form of memories and can be brought to our conscious mind by retrieving them—by thinking about them.

Another interesting fact is that all our experiences are attached with emotions, which we go through at the time of the incident or experience. When a memory comes to our conscious awareness, the emotions automatically come alive. The idea behind reliving the past is to retrieve the negative or fear-based emotions that are stored in the subconscious mind and bring them to the conscious mind where they can be addressed and processed.

Why do we need to address these emotions? These negative emotions play havoc in our present life, affecting our decision-making abilities, our health, our relationships, our professional life, our day-to-day dealings with people and more importantly, our progress. They stop us from developing our full potential, depriving us from becoming who we truly are capable of becoming—happy and successful individuals.

Sometimes it is easy to recall bad experiences of the past, depending on the intensity and the time of the experience. Other times, a situation or an event similar to the past experience acts as a trigger to remind us of it. Whatever the cause may be, unless we identify and get rid of these negative emotions, we cannot lead a completely happy life. Therefore, it is crucial to revisit memories with negative emotions and relive them, so we can release those emotions and be relieved. And this forms the basis of *relive to relieve*.

By reliving a particular experience from the past, we actually release the blocked traumas or emotions associated with that particular memory or incident. If we can somehow go back to that incident and relive it in our minds, we can release the trauma and relieve ourselves from the effect of that trauma in the present moment. When we revisit these memories, they come to our conscious awareness or conscious mind where they can be processed and healed. Once the emotions are taken care of or released, the memory is automatically healed.

CLOSURE

Many times, people try to hide their true selves behind a mask, which does not suit them at all. But life has put them through such bad experiences that they find it easier to be in a disguise, as in the case of Maddie. She was 19 years old when she lost her parents in an accident. This incident changed her life completely, shattering all her dreams of a beautiful future. Over the next few years, she went through many difficulties and these turned her into someone she barely identified with. By nature Maddie was a very fun-loving and humorous girl, always full of smiles and laughter. But that was all in the past; now she lived life as an angry, fearful, and self-doubting adult.

When she came to me for therapy, I asked her to narrate the whole accident. The more Maddie tried to think about the incident, the more bitter she became. I realized that because the whole incident was unexpected, she could not have closure in the relationship with her parents and many things were unsaid. During the session, she had the opportunity to relive that memory and she could speak to her parents about all the things that she had wanted to, during the funeral. When she was ready, she bid them farewell and let them go.

Reliving this experience was painful to begin with, but once Maddie had received closure with what was left unsaid, she released that painful emotion attached to the memory. As a result, the memory was completely healed.

HEALING WOUNDS

When a wound is deep-rooted, treating it on the surface is a superficial or temporary measure, as the problem lies deep within. To heal the wound completely, the root cause needs to be treated; the wound will then heal and all that will be left is a faint scar. Yes, the scar is a reminder of the wound, but it won't be painful. The memories of our past with negative emotions are exactly like that. Once we have retrieved, processed, and released the negative emotions, they are healed. The memory of the experience will remain, but will not hurt or cause pain.

Linda was a natural host, who enjoyed planning and hosting parties, get-togethers, and charity events. Her extroverted personality and go-getter attitude drew the respect of all in her community. She was always the leader and center of attention. Everything was going great for her family, until her husband lost his job. The global recession had set in and Linda's husband was one of the many victims.

When he lost his job of twenty years, it was a hard blow for the entire family. He was a good person, but losing the job was a very difficult thing for him to accept, especially at his age. Soon he lost touch with his friends and confined himself to his room. Linda realized that her husband was in depression and tried everything possible to be supportive and pull him out of his vacuum. But nothing worked; it was painful for her to see her husband sit quietly in a corner and do absolutely nothing.

One day a family friend informed Linda that there was a good job opening for her husband and he should go for the interview immediately. Linda was very excited, but her husband was not. After much persuasion, Linda finally fought with him and forced him to go for the interview. A couple of hours later, the police called to inform her that her husband had met with a fatal accident on the highway. The police had traced Linda's whereabouts from the victim's belongings.

Six years after this unfortunate incident, Linda came to me for a therapy session. It was clear that she was living in guilt as she held herself responsible for her husband's death. During the session, Linda was able to relive the entire episode, release the pain, and forgive herself. She accepted that it was an accident and she had nothing to do with his death and slowly she was able to move on.

The tragic death of a loved one causes immense pain, anger, and bitterness. In Linda's case, in addition to the pain of losing a loved one, she also felt guilty for believing that she was the reason behind it. I would like to point out here that healing is a process; and it takes time. We have to be prepared to let go of the painful emotions attached to an experience.

It is only when you are ready, that you can actually release that pain. What you have to understand and accept is that you have no control over something that has already happened.

Nothing can change the past. But your willingness to let go definitely helps relieve the traumas. You can surely give this gift to yourself.

Our minds are more powerful than we can imagine. It stores every single incident that has ever taken place in our lives, like a master computer. What we may think as "forgotten" is never so. And at any point in time, we can retrieve the data, by metaphorically logging into it. However, sometimes it may seem impossible as we may not recall anything that happened to us at a young age. But just because we don't remember, does not mean it is not there!

THOUGHTS

_____

_____

_____

Memories exist in our present-day life through the behavior, action, and attitude we display. Most of the time we may behave in a particular way, which is in contrast to who we really are. Many times people around us and we ourselves may not understand why we behave the way we do. This is because many of us are not aware that the behavior is streaming from deep within our subconscious minds.

Certain things never really leave us. When we revisit the memories and live them again as if the events were taking place in the present, we actually release the emotions and traumas attached to those memories. The process is simple. We just need to bring the subconscious memories to the conscious mind and then experience each and every emotion we had experienced at the time of that incident. This process is also called catharsis or cleansing. By doing so, we are getting a second chance to have closure.

It is very important that we have closure, for our sakes as well as our loved ones' sake. Nothing is gone until we completely *allow* it to be gone. And when we let go of a traumatic event from the past, we heal inward and allow ourselves to be healthier and happier people.

Have you ever noticed how, while reading a book, sometimes we want to go back to the pages that we have already read? As if we have missed something important, as if something within us had urged us to reread a particular part of the book? When we go back to that chapter and read it again, we feel a sense of completeness, and then we are able to continue reading the rest of the book peacefully and happily.

It's the same with life. Our life is a great story with so many mysteries ahead, but until we completely let go of the traumatic past memories, rooted deep in our subconscious mind, we will not be able to continue the rest of the story happily. When we have an option to live a better life, why choose a bitter one?

The reason I emphasize reliving is because the root cause and the solution to most of our problems lie within us. But since we are unaware, we are unable to do anything about it. Sometimes the answers are right there at the back of our minds, safely and secretly stored away, without us even knowing that they exist.

Given a chance, everyone would like to let go completely of the traumas and negative emotions of the past. Given a chance, we would like to be completely happy and carefree. Given a chance, we would like to edit the script of our lives to ensure a happy ending. The question is, is it possible? Yes, of course it is! And the key to unlock the demons and monsters and destroy them lies in our hands.

Let's give ourselves a second chance to live the life that truly represents us.

AT A GLANCE

- By reliving a past incident mentally, you can release attached negative emotions.

- It is important to have closure with the past.

- You must be willingly ready to let go.

CHAPTER 5

YOUR INNER CHILD— THE FOUNTAIN OF JOY

I want to dance in rain, blow bubbles of soap;
I am the inner child, full of life and hope.
I like to run and play and shout and sing
And scream with joy, as if no one's listening.

One evening I came home from work extremely stressed and angry. At that time, I was still working in the corporate setup. I'm not the sort of person who gets angry easily, but that was an exceptional evening. The continuous traveling, endless meetings, reports, deadlines, and constant bickering from bosses had finally taken a toll on me. I entered my home in a rage and got into an argument with everyone.

That night I had no appetite, shunned dinner, and asked everyone to leave me alone. As I retired to bed late, I calmed down and started to question my behavior. I felt extremely guilty. The next morning, I began the damage control by apologizing to everyone.

As I drove to work, something inside me kept screaming to take a break. So that weekend, I decided to go alone for a nature walk to a forest near my home. I watched the sun rise, slowly turning the dark blue skies into a sweet orange color. I noticed how breathtakingly scenic the forest was as I walked leisurely, taking time to soak in the beauty of the place.

The aroma of the grass was sweet and the morning dew looked like tiny little pearls scattered all over each blade; the tall trees looked like giant guardians of the forest; the ground was filled with wild flowers of all kinds and colors creating a carpet woven on earth. The gentle sound of the stream flowing nearby felt like melody to accompany the singing of the birds that were chirping in chorus. It felt like the forest was welcoming me along with the dawn. I took a few deep breaths of the fresh air and stood still for a while, in awe of the beauty that surrounded me.

As I looked around, I spotted a bunch of beautiful butterflies sitting on a berry shrub. My first thought on seeing the butterflies was to run and catch them. But when I went near the shrub, they flew off. I looked around to see if anyone was watching me, and when I realized that I was alone, without wasting a second, I started running after them. The various colors of butterfly wings fluttering in the air were like hundreds of tiny rainbows forming momentarily in front of my eyes. It was simply an astonishing exhibition of life within nature. I ran behind them with all enthusiasm, going up and down the hillocks. After sometime, I stopped running and just watched them.

As I sat down, completely breathless, I laughed out loudly, dumbfounded by the beautiful display of life in front of my eyes. The experience was awesome and filled my heart with joy. Although I had been running after the butterflies, I was not tired; I felt fully energized and completely rejuvenated. I relaxed in the lap of nature, and it struck me that I had gone back in time to when I was ten years old.

As a kid, I used to enjoy chasing butterflies in the hope of catching one. I had not run like that since I was a kid. This experience completely rejuvenated me and brought back so many wonderful childhood memories. I had reconnected to the inner child in me. The inner child was always inside me, but ignored for too long. This newfound enthusiasm was because I had allowed the inner child to come out and take over the adult in me.

Can you recollect similar incidents that gave you tremendous joy as a child? Things you thoroughly enjoyed doing and had enormous amounts of fun with, like catching ladybugs, climbing trees, plucking berries, eating raw fruit, getting drenched and dancing in the rain, playing hide and seek, playing football or soccer in the mud, playing with dolls or trucks, hiding under the bed, coloring, making a wish then blowing out the candles on your birthday cake, bursting balloons, licking ice cream off your fingers, wrists, and elbows as it melts, making sand castles, collecting sea shells or stamps, blowing soap bubbles, building a castle with cards....

THOUGHTS

_____

_____

_____

The list is endless. Just making a list of the fun things will bring back such wonderful and joyous memories. Imagine how much more fun you would have if you could actually do them again?

Do you remember how excited you were blowing out the candles on your birthday? Being the center of attention, everyone singing the happy birthday song for you while you smiled from ear to ear, waiting to cut the cake. The cake cutting was such a _wow_ moment. It was the moment you waited for the entire time, followed by the birthday gifts that you received with a big "Thank you," and tore open the wrapping paper, to unveil the delights that were yours. Those were such fun, simple, and exciting days.

But times have changed; you grew up and became a responsible adult. For some, it would be embarrassing if people found out they were excited about a simple thing as a birthday. Some adults even find it a total waste of time.

I vividly remember that, as a little boy, I enjoyed lying on the floor and watching an army of ants march in a single neat file carrying sugar and disappear into a crevice. I watched them with awe and curiosity and wondered where they lived. I really enjoyed doing that. I wonder how my wife would react if I were to do that now.

As children we were so innocent, we had so much fun doing simple things, like running around aimlessly or screaming at top of our voices. As years went by, we stopped doing these things and grew up into so-called "responsible adults." It is as if a rule book of dos and don'ts was handed over to us and all the fun things we liked was listed under the don'ts. It would be considered absolutely crazy if we were caught doing anything childlike, or as we so often hear people say "childish."

Funnily enough, as "sensible adults," we see the same army of ants as harmful pests. It's not that the ants have changed, but our outlook toward them definitely has. The point is we no longer connect to the ants in the same way or for that matter to any of the simple things that we used to as children. And that is because we are no longer connected to the inner child within our hearts.

THE CHILD WITHIN

The inner child is the little child we were, who still resides within us, who desires to be nurtured, cared for, and loved. It is the fun-loving, happy, joyful, humorous *us* when we were young. It is also the emotional, sensitive, creative, and imaginative *us* whom we have controlled and silenced. It is a part of *us* that is hurt, neglected, abused, ignored, and hidden from view. This child is just below the surface, causing us to be anxious, worried, and fearful of mistreatment.

The inner child is the part of us who was left behind somewhere, who never grew up—although the other part of us did physically grow up. Our inner child is simply defined by the qualities it represents and the behavior it exhibits, such as joy, freedom of expression, fearlessness, honesty, trust, carefree, spontaneity, mischief, etc. All these and many more positive characteristics combined are a true portrayal of our inner child.

However, these attributes start disappearing slowly from our lives as we grow up, and other new ones cover them, completely redefining our personality. This is similar to a sunken boat becoming covered with layers of algae.

It is possible to know whether our inner child is active or not. If we 1) lose ourselves in children's fun activities or enjoy playing with children's toys; or 2) cry during an emotional movie; or 3) overindulge with our own children; or 4) love visiting theme parks designed for children; or 5) get emotional looking at old photo albums, home movies, or scrapbooks from our childhood, or even 6) seek to please the senior members of our families—then our inner child is still active and we should try to keep in touch with that deeper part of us.

The inner child exists in our subconscious minds. It is a concept used in psychology to indicate the innocent, childlike part of human mind. The term is often used to talk about someone's experiences during childhood and its residual effects. We can clearly picture what the little child looks like and how the child is feeling and acting.

Over the years, memories stored in our subconscious minds, the layers of conditioning, the belief systems, and the excess baggage of negative emotions such as bitterness, pain, anger, guilt, resentment, and fear, act as knives that gradually cut us away from our inner child. It is important to note here that this transition varies from person to person. That is because every individual is different—the experience is different and the ability to deal with a particular situation is also different, depending on the circumstances.

Societal norms, family values, belief systems, social and financial stratum, and many other factors play a great role in shaping an individual. The inner child comes into being by our denial of our true feelings, especially when we try hard to live up to others' expectations. In doing so, we hold back our childlike responses, thinking that we always have to be "serious" about life. We do not feel the freedom to play and act childish. We feel that we are being loved for what we do rather than who we are.

KAVYA'S LOSS

Kavya was a young girl of twenty when she was married, and a true example of a person who was in touch with her inner child. Her days were filled with laughter, jokes, and stories. There was never a dull moment in her life. She paid no heed to people who made fun of her childlike behavior. Those who resonated with her found her full of positive energy and life. She was the star of every picnic and party, and children loved to play with her.

After three years of marriage, Kavya had a baby. Her pregnancy was not a smooth one. During that time elderly ladies, with many years of experience and full of strict rules surrounded her. She was soon restricted from doing many things she enjoyed, but she had no choice but to follow.

Her husband noticed the first changes in her behavior and attitude toward people and situations. Her opinions were different; she no longer laughed out loud, joked around, or enjoyed the simple things she liked. He took this as a phase that would dissipate after the baby arrived. The arrival of the baby was a joyous moment for all in the family.

The new mother was happy, but not cheerful or excited. I once asked her why she was not her old bubbly self, to which she replied, "I'm no longer a kid, I'm a mother now, and can't behave like a child anymore!"

Gradually, she distanced herself from her inner child and donned a new role of mother. It's a beautiful thing to be a mother; in fact, it is one of most delightful miracles in the world. But that does not mean you have to disconnect from your inner child!

What do you think happened to that child in you? The child who was the real you, the child who was full of dreams, the child who was afraid of nothing, the child who was willing to take on risks and adventures, the child who laughed and screamed and ran. Most of us look back at those good old childhood days with fond memories, but say, "Well I'm all grown up. I'm an adult now, I have responsibilities. I have so much to do, bills to pay, errands to run, reports to complete. I have a duty toward my company, my family, the society. I cannot sit around and blow bubbles all day, that's crazy and ridiculous!"

If this is what our answer is, then it confirms only one thing. We no longer feel connected to our inner child. This is because we have ignored that child and are not connected with it, we don't believe it exists. But that child is very much alive. In fact, that child is screaming to get out and be acknowledged. That inner child that we have ignored for so long is the solution to many of our setbacks in life today.

What has changed? As we grow up, various changes take place in our lives. The additional responsibilities, change of role, change of place, various incidents, our societal conditioning. Like when we are told:

"Stop behaving like a child, you are a grown-up now."

"You have to study hard and get excellent grades."

"You must get into the best college."

"You must earn at least a six-figure salary."

"You must join an international company."

"You must get married now."

"You must have a child now."

The endless list of do's and don'ts handed down while growing up, gradually and unconsciously, distance us from our inner child. Sometimes, resentment toward the people who have stopped us from doing what we really enjoyed as children also acts as a barrier between us and the inner child. More so if those people are still in our lives.

And when we are no longer connected to that inner child, we no longer feel its presence in our lives, and when we no longer identify with it, we draw an iron curtain between the adult and the inner child. Then comes a time when we refuse to acknowledge the existence of that inner child altogether.

The inner child is the part of us that is not complete. It is part of our being, which we have left somewhere in the past, in the process of growing up. The inner child is ignored and deprived of doing what it enjoys most and that's why we often feel incomplete as adults. This incomplete part of us, unless healed or attended to, creates an unfulfilled life. It often pulls us back from the path of our success. But we can reconnect to our inner child anywhere, any place, any time. We just need to be willing to do so.

TIPS TO HEAL THE INNER CHILD

The first step toward healing our inner child is to acknowledge that we are disconnected from it. We have to recognize the problem in order to find a solution for it. Here are few questions we can ask ourselves:

• Do I often feel irritated, sad, angry, sacred, or shy?

• Am I unhappy in my relationships?

• Do I fail to express myself openly?

• Do I have low self-esteem?

• Do I often feel hurt?

• Do I often feel angry or jealous?

If most answers are yes, this validates that our inner child is hurt and has been ignored for a long time. Our current state of life and the behavior we exhibit determines the extent of damage to the inner child.

Acknowledging the problem is only the tip of the iceberg. The real and important step to healing the inner child is to identify the cause. If the inner child is hurt or damaged, then the adult, who carries this inner child, will be living in resentment, anger, pain and fear. We need to go back to our early childhood days and slowly walk through, step by step, carefully identifying the issues, events, and people who were instrumental in hurting or causing damage to our inner child. For example, if as a child we were loud, always laughing and shouting, but were constantly reprimanded for that behavior, we were slowly conditioned to believe that speaking or laughing loudly is considered bad behavior. And as a result we grew into adults abiding by that erroneous assumption; and more so, we now advocate it to others.

Once we have identified the reasons for ignoring our inner child, the next step is to accept. Accept that our inner child is hurt or has been disconnected. Accept that the past cannot be changed; however, it can definitely be healed. The healing can only take place when we whole-heartedly and honestly accept ourselves with all our flaws.

Acceptance forms an essential part of the healing process of the inner child. It is okay to feel angry, hurt, that we have been ignored. Remember that healing will not happen overnight, just as the damage was not caused overnight. We have to be patient with ourselves and give ourselves the time to heal.

After we have accepted the traumas our inner child has gone through, it's time to release those traumas and reconnect to the inner child. Talk to the inner child! Find out what is that one thing that would really make us happy. There is a simple yet beautiful process through which we can analyze why and under what circumstance we have drawn the curtain between the inner child and ourselves.

Once we are able to identify that block, that fear, which is holding back the inner child in us, we will find new energy and enthusiasm, like I felt that day in the forest. By being connected to our inner child, we can overcome the fears we are harboring, explore our true potential with new horizons, and succeed at anything we always wanted to achieve.

AT A GLANCE

- There is a child in you.

- You disconnected yourself from your inner child as you grew up.

- One of the main reasons for your misery is this disconnect.

- You must try to reconnect to that inner child.

CHAPTER 6
THE GIFT OF FORGIVENESS

I want to be free from guilt of the past,
My anger and regrets and shadows they cast.
I want to forgive and let go once and for all
It's for my own self, and I must take the call.

SET YOURSELF FREE

A few months back, I met an old friend. He had come to town for some work and we decided to have lunch. As we were eating, he suddenly said, "It doesn't pay to be honest, the world is full of crooks, and one needs to be manipulative."

Five years back, Sam had been falsely accused of taking a favor and asked to resign from a company that he served for fifteen years with honesty and dedication. Sam was a hard-working and honest guy. I could see that he still suffered from that incident. He was hurt and depressed and this was affecting his present life, both at work and home.

With great difficulty, I talked him into attending one of my workshops. After the first day of the workshop, I made him talk to me about what was bothering him. After he poured his heart out, I asked him to write down everything he felt, especially the names of all the people who had hurt him. An hour later, he had filled pages.

After taking a look at his "released rage," I said, "Sam, you are filled with so much hurt, anger, and bitterness. Do you realize that by constantly talking about them you are still connected to all those people involved with the incident? If you wish to live a happy life, you need to forgive. It may not be easy, but it is possible. Until you have forgiven, you will not be able to move on. The choice is yours; do you want to carry the entire burden around? Or leave it behind right now?"

Sam seemed quite eager to leave it all behind. I asked him to tear up the papers on which he had written down all his troubles and burn it. I told him to forgive each and every person from the bottom of his heart while doing this exercise. After a month when I met him again, I saw in him my old college friend, the one who was cheerful and happy.

CUTTING THE STRINGS

Forgiveness is the sword that cuts the ropes of bondage of our past negative emotions that we unconsciously carry, day in and day out. Forgiveness is a conscious decision to let go of resentment and thoughts of revenge. The experience that hurt or upset us might always remain a part of our lives, but by forgiving we will lessen the grip it has on us. This allows us to focus on other positive aspects of life.

Forgiveness is a tool that sets us free to soar high toward our ambitions, without the heavy baggage of our negative emotions. Forgiveness helps us disconnect from our past bad experiences and the emotions set therein. This helps us move toward our ultimate goal or purpose of life. It is through forgiveness that we open the cage, in which we are trapped, to set ourselves free. When we forgive, we have closure for the unresolved issues of the past. Forgiveness can even lead to feelings of understanding, empathy, and compassion for the one who hurt us.

Forgiveness doesn't mean that we deny the other person's responsibility for hurting us, and it doesn't minimize or justify the wrong. By forgiving, we are not condoning or approving the act itself. We are releasing ourselves from that hurt. The person we find most difficult to forgive, is the one we have to let go of the most. Forgiveness brings a special kind of peace that helps us go on with life.

Many of us can relate to the irritation caused by a dust particle in the eye, especially when we are in the midst of something important. We stop whatever we are doing and try all kinds of remedies to get rid of that tiny particle that's bothering us. Until that happens, we can't see clearly. And only when we see clearly, can we focus.

The anger, the irritation, and the discomfort we feel at that moment due to that tiny dust particle is minuscule compared to the burden and hurt we have been carrying for years because we have not forgiven. It is like thousands of tiny dust particles getting into our eyes and putting us through unbearable pain and discomfort.

Are we willing to undergo that cleansing, get rid of that burden, so that our vision is clear and we can focus on the present and future ahead? If we are ready, then it is time to forgive.

THOUGHTS

_____

_____

_____

Forgiving and letting go is all about you. It is about making peace with your inner self. Even science attests to this phenomenon. As per some studies, when you forgive from the heart, certain hormones are released from your endocrine system that are extremely beneficial for your health and well-being. When you forgive completely and from your heart, the reminiscence of negative emotions is wiped from your being.

THE CRYSTAL VASE

We often live in pain and guilt because we hold our loved ones responsible for trivial issues, and carry that burden for years.

One day while playing in the house, Mary and her brothers broke an expensive crystal vase. The eldest of the three siblings, Mary, stood still with fear along with her younger brothers Jim and James. Her mother, Jane, came running into the living room, looked at the broken vase and started crying. "I'm sorry, Mum," said Mary. Her mother went over to Mary and slapped her.

This was a very special vase; it was a gift from Mary's father, who had died a year earlier. The loss of her husband, little money, and three kids to care for had turned Jane into a bitter widow.

Jane collected the broken pieces, while crying, and kept them in a box. Then she looked into the little girl's eyes with anger and said, "You have broken something very precious and it can never be replaced. I used to think of him all the time looking at the vase, and now it is gone. I will never forgive you for this, Mary."

Years passed, but the relationship between Mary and her mother was never the same again. Jane always found a reason to be nasty to Mary, and Mary knew why, but never said anything. Jane had been living alone since the kids had moved out. One day she got a call informing her that Mary had an accident.

When Jane arrived at the hospital, both her sons and Mary's husband were waiting for her. Jane's son, James, informed her that Mary was in very bad condition and that she might not survive. Jane went into Mary's room and sat near her bed. For the first time in many years, Jane started to cry. As she held her only daughter's hand, Mary slowly opened her eyes and smiled. "Don't cry, Mum," she said in a feeble voice. "I'm not in pain, I'm glad you came. Please forgive me for the vase; I know you have been upset with me all these years."

Jane, still crying, kissed her daughter's hand and said, "I love you honey, and I know I haven't been fair to you, I forgive you. I forgive you completely, and I know it was an accident."

Mary passed away peacefully in her sleep, the next day. After the funeral was over, James informed his mother that it was he who had broken the vase that day. Jane had forgiven her daughter, but she still had to forgive herself. Sometimes we carry burdens that we realize after many years were just not worth it.

Forgiveness is the act of releasing ourselves from a painful burden—a burden that we carry for years that weighs us down. Unforgiveness leaves us standing miles away from where we could have reached in life, had we forgiven. When we release this burden, we have made peace with the pain and are ready to let go.

KARISHMA'S PLIGHT

Until we are at peace with ourselves, the burden follows us everywhere in life as a ghost, as in the case of Karishma. Karishma and her mother-in-law never agreed on anything. This caused many fights and gradually created an iron wall between them that was never broken down.

Recently during dinner at her best friend's place, Karishma talked about how her mother-in-law would have found fault in each and every thing—from the dinner menu to the décor, to the people who were invited.

Her friend listened to her with patience and said, "Karishma, she's been dead for three years now. I feel you need to just forgive her and put an end to this constant bickering. It's almost like you carry her around wherever you go. It's not healthy at all. You become so bitter and angry each time you speak of her. Talking about all the wrong things she said or did won't change anything now. She's gone, make peace with her at least now. Let her go."

That night Karishma went home and cried her heart out while recalling all the things her mother-in-law had said or done to hurt her. After crying for a long time, she went outside and looked at the sky and said aloud, "I forgive you unconditionally for all the hurt and pain you have caused me. I release you from my life right now. I've made peace with the hurt and pain that you caused me. Rest in peace, I forgive you!"

Sometimes intervention is highly important in the process of forgiveness. Most often we are not even conscious that we are carrying so much hurt and pain from the past, like in the case of Karishma. Only when her friend pointed it out did she realize the burden she had been carrying all along.

Understanding why we need to forgive is 80 percent of the job done. This involves a continuous introspection. The balance 20 percent is the actual act of forgiveness. When we understand, forgiving becomes very simple. Only when we forgive 100 percent do we grow into happy and complete individuals.

Have you ever observed how many times we say "Sorry" in a day? Now think, how many times do we really mean it? Asking for forgiveness is equally important and plays a huge role in living a fulfilled life.

GIVE YOURSELF THE GIFT OF FORGIVENESS

Guilt is an emotion that we experience when we hurt someone. It is a heavy burden to carry around day in, day out. It starts showing very quickly in our behavior toward everything in life. We tend to give justifications for everything or become extremely defensive. This behavior arises, most often, out of guilt. Most of the time we are not able to relate to this pattern of behavior or connect to the guilt inside us, and hence continue living in ignorance.

Living with guilt is like allowing a poisonous creeper to grow around a healthy plant. No matter how much you trim it, it will grow back again and eventually engulf and kill the plant itself. This is how guilt works in our lives, like a poisonous creeper, preventing us from blossoming into beautiful and happy individuals and from achieving our true potential. What is important is to uproot the poisonous creeper from our lives completely and throw it as far away as possible.

Many times we don't find anything wrong, and assure ourselves that everything is fine. We convince ourselves that there is nothing to feel guilty about, or that we may have been too hard on ourselves. We conveniently ignore the guilt, which is like a deep-rooted wound that on the surface seems fine. But in truth, it is actually growing inside us and will eventually prove to be fatal, if not treated quickly.

First we need to acknowledge its existence, then confront it with courage, operate on it with faith, and treat it from the root. Once we have done that, we will feel liberated—as if a soothing lotion has been applied on the wound.

Like in the case of Jelita, whose father-in-law suffered a lot in the past five years of his life because he did not ask for forgiveness. Jelita did everything possible to be the perfect daughter-in-law. However, her father-in-law was always accusing her of something. As things got worse, Jelita and her husband moved out.

Jelita visited her in-laws regularly and never once complained or fought back. Deep in his heart the old man knew that Jelita was a nice girl, but his own awful nature compelled him to fight with her. He was always in and out of the hospitals, but the doctors couldn't diagnose any major problem. When the doctors finally saw the end coming, they informed his family members. The old man asked for a priest to come and pray for him.

As the priest prayed, the old man said, "Father, I want to be forgiven for all the wrong things I have done in this life." The priest said, "If you truly want to be forgiven, apologize to the ones you have hurt."

After a lot of contemplation and hesitation, the old man asked to speak to Jelita. He said to her, "I know I have been mean to you all my life. I have intentionally said and done so many things to hurt you. I have also made you cry. And I know that today I suffer because of my own deeds. I'm so sorry, Jelita, I beg you to forgive me. I can't take this burden anymore."

Jelita accepted the old man's apology and said that she had completely forgiven him. In his last few days, the old man was full of life. He joked and laughed with all who came to visit him. It was astonishing how much he had changed from the old, mean, and grumpy man he was. He died in peace.

The act of apologizing, saying "I'm sorry," is an overwhelming feeling. It releases us from an iron cage in which we have been trapped for years. Only those who have had the courage to ask for forgiveness can relate to it. However, remember not to attach any expectations to it because there is no guarantee that the other person will forgive, and there is no point questioning why we are not forgiven. What is important is that we are willing to ask for forgiveness. And just by doing that we are released from the guilt that we harbor inside.

What is more important is that we are healed and ready to move on to achieve our full potential. That is the miracle of forgiving and asking to be forgiven. Both are life-changing virtues and lead to greater spiritual and psychological well-being and healthier relationships. The result is a life of less anxiety, stress, and hostility, which are the root causes of hypertension and depression.

We always have a choice, and we can either choose to live a life filled with hurt, anger, and guilt, or we can choose to forgive and see our true self blossom.

AT A GLANCE

- Forgiveness is the tool you can use to cut the strings of the past.

- Forgiveness releases you from a painful burden.

- Forgiveness is about making peace with yourself.

- Forgiveness is only about you—to let go and move on.

- You always have a choice—to forgive and forget.

CHAPTER 7

HEALING YOUR PAST

HAVE YOU HEALED YOUR PAST ENOUGH?

Every person has a past. As we move ahead in time, the preceding moment becomes the past. The unresolved emotions from the past pull us back, depriving us of the joy of present and the zest for the future. It is extremely important to assess ourselves from time to time, to know if we have completely healed our past.

This chapter offers a small exercise to help you analyze how healed from the past you are. Take some time out for yourself and find a quiet place. You can listen to some nice, relaxing music. Just shut yourself off from all sorts of disturbances and outside noise. Switch off your mobile phone, put off your doorbell, and make sure that nobody disturbs you.

All you need for this exercise is a pen or pencil. You can also use blank sheets of paper. When you start the exercise, you need to be honest with your answers. Take time to think.

Answer the following questions with *Yes* or *No*—not *Maybe*. You can also note certain incidents from the past that triggered your answers or certain issues you feel you need to resolve. Make a note of it on the blank sheets.

After you finish the exercise, go back to these notes and try to resolve or heal them one by one using the "powerful tools to heal your past" given in the next chapter.

Delving into your past is a valuable gift you are giving yourself. So, get ready, get set…go!

1. Do you try to avoid talking about your past?

2. Do you think any conditioning or belief system is stopping you from doing what you like?

3. If someone makes you angry or upset, do you go down memory lane and recall all the times this person made you feel like this?

4. When you are alone and think about unhappy past incidents, do you get upset?

5. Do you feel guilty about something that happened in the past?

6. Do failures in the past stop you from taking steps toward new ventures?

7. Are you afraid of taking risks?

8. Do the traumatic incidents in your past still haunt you?

9. Do you blame others for your current situation in your life?

10. Is it difficult for you to let go and move on?

11. Are you afraid to recall and resolve traumatic memories?

12. Do you resist doing something that you enjoyed doing as a child?

13. Is there anything you have done in the past for which you have not completely forgiven yourself?

14. Is there anyone you have still not forgiven for hurting you in the past?

15. Do you see yourself as the same person today as you were in the past?

If the answer to 10 or more of these questions is *No*, then congratulations! You are on a forward journey in life. You just need to consciously continue the healing process to keep yourself healed of your past. However, if 10 or more of your answers are *Yes*, then you have a second chance right now to heal your past.

After you finish assessing, revisit the questions where the answer is *Yes*, refer to the notes you have made and work on them with the tools given in the next chapter.

CHAPTER 8

POWERFUL TOOLS TO HEAL YOURSELF

The following are twelve tried and tested powerful tools that will help you heal your past.

Relieve through forgiveness. Visualize any painful or traumatic incident of the past that you need to heal, as if it is happening in the present. Imagine that incident in the smallest possible detail; for example, what time of the day it was, who were the people present, the location, what were the feelings the incident generated, etc. Get into all the details of that incident. Feel all the negative emotions you felt at that time. Acknowledge them. If you feel like crying, that's fine. Let all the emotions flow out. If you are feeling guilt, ask for forgiveness from those whom you have wronged. See that they have forgiven you. Remember, it is important to ask for forgiveness. Just asking for forgiveness relieves you of the burden you are carrying.

It is also important to forgive yourself completely. Similarly, if you were emotionally hurt in a past incident, forgive all the people who have hurt you. You need to move on. This exercise will help offload a lot of emotions that pull you back, such as anger, guilt, remorse, hatred, sorrow, etc. It is possible to heal yourself from any of your past traumatic incidents, even if it involves people who have since departed. The basic prerequisite for this exercise is that you should be willing to let go, through forgiving or asking for forgiveness. Visualizing a painful memory in its complete detail as if it is happening in the present, helps to bring the memory to your conscious mind. This helps in relieving the painful emotions through reliving the past memory.

Make a list. Make a list of all the people, places, things, and incidents that bother you. For each on the list, write what is it that bothers you. Once you've written it down, tear the paper into small pieces and say, "I let go" while tearing. Afterward, flush or burn the pieces. Repeat this exercise for seven days and you will see the result yourself.

Cutting the Cord. Cutting the cord is a very powerful tool. Visualize that there is an invisible cord that connects you and the person whom you would like to let go of from your life. Feel the connection with that person through this cord. Ask the universe to give you an imaginary pair of scissors and imagine a pair of scissors being placed in your hands. Now with these pair of scissors, cut the imaginary cord and see the person moving away from you to his or her own journey. Thank the person for the role he or she played in your life and for teaching you valuable life lessons. The person you imagine could be living or even departed. This can also be done for a situation. Sometimes you are too attached to a negative situation from the past that haunts you. For example, you could be a witness to some tragic incident, such as an accident, riots, etc. In this case, treat the situation as an entity and repeat the cord-cutting exercise.

The **HOPE** (Hold On to Positive Empowerment) **Technique**. Sit in a comfortable position and close your eyes and breathe as deeply as you can. Concentrate on each breath and count 15 to 20 breaths. Now lightly tap on your left shoulder with right hand. As you tap, think of one or more of your painful or negative memories. Visualize them filling the left side of your body. Feel the pain or traumatic emotions due to those memories as you do so. Then with your left hand, lightly tap the right shoulder. As you tap, think of one or more of your most positive or happy memories. Visualize them filling the right side of your body. Feel the happiness or positive emotions due to these memories as they come out. Now again tap the left shoulder with the right hand, and see all the negative emotions and memories flowing like liquid out of your left hand and fingers and absorbed by the earth. Feel the vacuum created in the left side of your body due to this. Now tap the right shoulder and see the positive emotions in the right part of your body filling the entire space in your body. Feel the positive emotions, happiness, joy, courage, love, confidence, peace, etc. filling in your whole body.

Then visualize any symbol in front of your eyes, it could be any shape and color of your choice, or a positive symbol you associate yourself with. Now repeat the affirmation three times, "This symbol fills me with all positive emotions" and open your eyes. Whenever you feel troubled with any negative emotions related to the past, you can remember this symbol and can feel yourself being filled with positive emotions. This symbol could even be a sound or a certain word, or just a deep breath. This technique is called HOPE (Hold On to Positive Empowerment), because you can use this any time to come out of negative emotions and instantly feel positive and happy.

Banish clutter. Cleaning your house of clutter is a very easy and quick way to heal yourself. The old, broken things in the house may carry emotions associated with a traumatic memory in the past. Many times just looking at something causes your mind to be flooded with unpleasant incidents or memories, which then causes a chain reaction leading to completely unrelated but negative memories as well. It helps to get rid of all the old, soiled, and broken articles in your house that are connected to such memories. You can immediately start feeling lighter by doing this.

Change of scenery. A change of house or town may also help to move away from a bad past and help heal faster. It also metaphorically means you are moving on and leaving unwanted baggage in the past.

Make amends. If you have not been in touch with someone over the years due to some misunderstanding in the past, take the initiative to call the person and clear up the misunderstanding. If you have to say sorry, then do so. If someone apologizes, accept it gracefully. The idea is to shed the baggage and move on. It really does not help us in the long run to keep misunderstandings or grudges in mind. What matters is being free to move forward. We must put a logical end to any such past emotional baggage to travel ahead lighter.

Explore like a child. Make a point to try something new every day. It could be a small thing, but has to be something you have never done before. Try anything new: a new route to the office, a new person to speak to, a new thing or word or phrase to learn. You can even do something that you have been doing for years, in a new way. This exercise frees you from the bondage of "should" and "should not." These should and should-not become part of our conditioning and play a major role in forming belief systems. The point is to break out of conditioning layers and patterns. Be good in experimenting.

Do what you enjoyed in the past. Many times we grow old very fast and label certain things as childish that we used to enjoy doing once upon a time. If doing a certain thing gave you happiness when you were a child, it will surely make you happy even now. The secret is to keep your inner child happy. Go ahead and blow soap bubbles, make castles in the sand, make paper boats or airplanes, climb trees, dance in the rain, or do anything that you loved doing as a child.

Spend time with children. Children connect us to our own childhood. The more time we spend with them, the happier we feel overall. It helps us to shed our inhibitions about doing certain things, which has probably been built over the years, knowingly or unknowingly. This exercise also brings out the inner child in us.

Pamper yourself. When something goes wrong we hold ourselves responsible and bury ourselves under a heap of guilt, anger, fear, hatred, jealousy, and resentment. We also punish ourselves at times and engage in self-sabotage, which ultimately adversely affects our self-esteem. This process needs to be reversed. Tell yourself, "It's ok," and move on. Pampering yourself in whatever way you can helps in moving on. Go and have an ice cream cone or pat yourself on the back. You can even buy yourself a gift or give yourself a spa treatment. You can find creative ways to pamper yourself. The underlying rule is, whatever makes you feel the best.

Positive Affirmations. Positive affirmations are like having an energy drink. They fill you with instant energy. Each time a negative thought comes to your mind just drink a thought of positive affirmation and recharge yourself. Here are a few affirmation statements to help you in the process of healing the past.

- I love and accept myself the way I am.

- I let go of all my hurt, pain, fear, anger, and guilt.

- I completely forgive myself and others who have hurt me.

- I am always surrounded by loving and positive people.

- I am always divinely protected.

CONCLUSION

This chapter concludes the Key #1 section, Heal Your Past. The next key, Key #2 Live Your Present, delves into important day-to-day attitudes, decisions, and purpose.

KEY #2

LIVE YOUR PRESENT

LIVE YOUR PRESENT

We must live our present, 'cause present is a gift
Living every moment, does make a deeper shift.
Each one of us has a life purpose, a task.
This is revealed to us whenever we ask.

Our purpose is hidden in things we love doing most
We must try to find that destination of life, at any cost.
Once we know the direction, we must start the walk
And leave it to the universe, to open our life's lock.

"Just do it" is the mantra that can take us ahead;
Get-up and get-going, and quickly leave the bed.
With no fear of taking risks, we'll certainly succeed,
Our passion giving us energy, and the courage that we need.

It doesn't really matter, what is our aptitude
The only thing that takes us far is our attitude.
Ships look great, while standing on the shore,
But that's not what ships are really made for.

Once we start walking, let's not stop for anything;
Let failures be our strength, to never give up and keep going.
This is the moment when we find our true happiness;
Choice lies with us, to live life large, or live less.

It's important to be thankful, for all we have in life,
Gratitude gives us the power to overcome our strife.
With our heads held high with towering self-esteem
Let's make our lives successful and achieve our dream.

This is the only moment when we can move ahead;
It's time to take action now, on whatever has been said.

CHAPTER 1

LIFE'S GREATEST GIFT— THE PRESENT MOMENT

Present is where life is, neither future nor past.
This is the moment where my destiny's die is cast.
Living in the now leads me to my peace
Where all my mind's chatter comes to cease.

When I bought my first car, I enrolled myself in a driving class. After three weeks of training and securing the driving license, it was time for me to hit the road on my own. I still remember the first day of driving independently, as that taught me life's greatest lesson.

I was able to drive smoothly on the highway, but as I turned onto a by-lane, the road went uphill. With the very sight of the incline, my pulse started racing. The traffic congestion was relatively high that day. The space between my car and the cars immediately front and behind was hardly a couple of meters.

Then my worst nightmare came true. As soon as I started going uphill, my car engine stopped and all my fears mushroomed inside me. Using my full presence of mind, I immediately applied pressure to the brake pedal. I had to restart the car to move ahead, so after turning on the ignition, I had to lift my foot off the brake and within a fraction of a second put it on accelerator and push it for the car to move ahead.

Now that was "the moment." If my attention shifted slightly from the present moment, my car would drift backward and bang into the car behind. So I had to be fully present in the moment. I realized that I was very anxious about the consequences before even taking the first step. I had to first calm myself down by taking few deep breaths, in the midst of honking car horns from behind. Then I gathered my consciousness to that moment and finally succeeded in moving the car ahead. I realized then what "living in the moment" was.

Most times, we either live in the past or in the future. It is as if we are driven by some mysterious compulsion to live through memories from the past or in anticipation of the future. These compulsions occur mainly because the past gives us an identity and the future holds promises. We either feel guilt or regret about the past, or worry or stress about the future; and thus completely miss the moment we are living— *the present moment.*

At every given moment we are climbing the uphill of life. There are many things from the past that pull us down, and believe me, it's very easy to be pulled backward as if on a slope. We can't even afford to stop; as a matter of fact, there is no way we can stop. If we don't push the accelerator every moment, there are all the chances of drifting backward, downhill. The real art lies in how successful we are present at that moment and move ahead without being pulled backward.

As a common saying goes, "The moments that are gone make the past, the moments that are yet to come is called future, but this particular moment, which is life, is called the present, the 'gift.'" It is only in this moment that we are living, we are alive. Both the past and the future are illusions, really. The *now* is all there is. Life is happening in this very moment. Life *is* the *present moment*. Every moment is an opportunity for us to create our future and at the same time define our past; as the present moment becomes the past the very next moment.

During an emergency or in the middle of life-threatening events, we are automatically living in the present. It is a natural process. Our personality, which contains our past and future, gives way to the present consciousness. Our response to the emergency situation then comes out of this state of present consciousness, which is extremely still and watchful at such times.

SUFFERING IS OPTIONAL

Kavita is a 35-year-old single woman who lives alone in the city. When I saw her after a long time, she looked completely worn down and visibly stressed out. "Is there something bothering you, Kavita?" I asked gently. She was stumped by my question, as she didn't expect it; she is the kind of person who usually puts on a brave face in public.

"How did you guess?" she exclaimed. With tear-filled eyes, she started to pour her heart out, "I feel very depressed and anxious nowadays. Do you have a solution for my problem?"

"Yes, I do," I said. "Just be."

Kavita seemed quite irritated by my suggestion. "You must be kidding!" she retorted. "My life has been very traumatic. I am haunted by the memories of my past. I am just not at peace with myself. I am now jobless and I don't know what's going to happen to me in future. And you are telling me to 'Just be'? That just sounds ridiculous to me."

It was clear to me that Kavita was purely exhausted by carrying so much baggage of her past memories. Since her mind was going through so much turbulence, she was also under a tight grip of fear and insecurity. I said to her, "Kavita, you are depressed because you are not letting go of your past baggage. And your anxiety is the result of your fears and insecurities about future. So you are either living in the past or in the future."

"So what do I do?" she asked.

"Just be, be present in the moment," I said. After a pause, I continued, "You see, only when you are in the moment can you get rid of stress, anxiety, and depression. You need to understand that the fears and insecurities about the future is only your projection. It is just an assumption. Whatever you fear about your future may or may not happen. It may just be your fears playing on your mind. It is not a reality."

I added, "Reality is only this moment, and in this moment you are just talking to me…that's it. These fears can be conquered by developing faith in yourself and trusting the process of life. Remember, your thoughts in this moment are going to create your future. If you have fears and insecurities about the future, it will eventually turn out to be that way. You are creating your future every moment."

I was glad to notice that Kavita was listening to me attentively. I continued, "Similarly your past is past…already gone. It no longer exists. It's a bygone. It exists only in your memory now. If those memories are haunting you, you need to handle them. Don't resist them. Accept those memories as part of your life… life you have lived. If they have caused you pain, you need to heal them. It is very important to protect and heal the wound with lots of self-love and forgiveness; otherwise, the wound becomes very vulnerable. Forgiveness is a very important healing tool. You need to forgive yourself for allowing people to hurt you."

Kavita was now completely immersed in self-introspection. She absorbed each and every word I was saying, "That's the reason I say, 'Just be.' By just being, you can handle all your issues in a better way. By being in the moment you are disconnecting yourself from the negative thoughts about the past or future. It is okay to feel hurt. But don't get attached to that hurt. Just experience it and move on. That is the beauty of being in the moment.

"Moreover, our thoughts have enormous power. They manifest, so scan every moment for the thought it is carrying. Every present moment is the vehicle for your thoughts. It has the power to swing you in any direction. So choose every thought very carefully. Appreciate every moment and be grateful for each moment. Being alive at every moment is itself a miracle," I told her.

"Thank you so much. I think I got it now. I'm really grateful to you for making me understand this," said Kavita with tears rolling down her cheeks, but with a peaceful and contented smile on her face.

Like Kavita, many people get so bogged down by the miseries of the past and the fears of the future that we refuse to live in the present moment. And when such a series of present moments pass away in front of our eyes, we say that our lives are full of misery. When the truth is, we created that life. As they say, "Pain is inevitable, but suffering is optional." The choice is all ours.

Many times it is our perspective toward life that makes us decide whether life has been fair or unfair. Look for beauty, and there it is—look for despair, and there it is! Even if there is a problem, the solution often lies in itself. We just need to introspect and discover it. There is no good or bad in life. It is a subjective term and is viewed in the perspective of time. Something which is good for someone can be bad for someone else. Or something bad in the present may turn out to be good in the future.

THOUGHTS

_____

_____

_____

Whenever we are not in the present moment, we are either in the past or in the future; and both are illusory, misleading. As a result, we totally miss the opportunities the present moment presents before us. We are actually unfair to ourselves by not being in the moment. We are depriving ourselves of the pure happiness that the present offers. The present moment is the only gateway through which we can go beyond the limited confines of the mind. This is where our complete life unfolds, and the only factor that remains constant. There was never a time, or will never be a time, when our life is not *now*.

BREATH BY BREATH

Breathing happens every moment. But unfortunately most often we are unaware of our breathing. We take our breaths for granted. When we are living in the past or for the future, thereby feeling depressed, angry, guilty, stressed, anxious, or fearful, our breathing changes rhythm or pattern. It becomes shallow and fast. If we become conscious of this change and then restore the rhythm by taking deep and slow breaths, we can instantly bring ourselves into the present moment. Being conscious about our breathing is the key.

Try to focus on breathing while taking slow, deeper breaths. Following your breath as it travels in and out of your body, feeling your abdomen expand and contract with each breath, is a great way to begin any meditation. The focus will then gently shift to your inner feelings. When we breathe in and out deeply and slowly, our awareness turns toward each breath and brings our attention to the present moment.

ILLUSIVE TIME

There is a fine difference between our perception of physical time and the illusive or mental time. Whenever we take note of our past events or apply the lessons learned from past mistakes in the present situation with positive feelings or heal our past in the present, we live in the physical time of *now*. However, when we dwell in the past mentally, letting the anger, guilt, remorse or self condemnation take over, we live in illusive time, which links us to a false identity.

Similarly, whenever we set targets or goals and work toward them, we again live in the physical present time. But if we are anxious about future events or gripped with fear, then we live in illusive time. There is nothing wrong in learning from past mistakes or healing the past and taking appropriate steps for the future by predicting from patterns or established laws—as long as we are doing this in the present or in the physical time of now.

Be careful of the slip from physical time into illusive time. When we live in illusive time, we do not take advantage of our full potential, which only comes out during the physical time of now. Try to let go of this tendency of unknowingly slipping into illusive time.

EXPERIENCING THE MOMENT

Many times rather than experiencing the present moment, we are either fast forwarding or going in reverse. For example, if we are late for a meeting, we will be completely disturbed

mentally. We are so anxious that our mind will either immediately rush to the future, thinking about the firing we may
receive from the boss, or thinking how we were late because of
morning issues at home. Either way, we are not living in the
moment and experiencing it as it is in the present.

We can learn to be in the moment and experience the present.
For that, we should first learn to free our minds of its habitual
caught-in-responsibility, self-absorbed, stress-filled state.

Sometimes the true value of the moment is never really appreciated or even known until it becomes a memory. We are all
running. We are either running toward our pleasure or we are
running toward acquiring more and more knowledge. It is important to be still sometimes and not run in either direction.

As an experiment, take a lunchtime walk to a park to feed the
birds or fish. Be so fascinated with the wildlife, their eating
habits, the other people feeding them, and the natural environment that you forget what just happened that morning and you
don't pre-think the afternoon. Your mind will relax, your heart
will relax, you'll smile at people, and they will smile back. Or on
your next coffee break, really take a break and just have coffee.
That's all. Don't talk on phone. Don't check emails. Don't visit
anyone. Just taste the coffee. Look around. See your surroundings as if for the first time—with wonder in your eyes.

Sometimes it is very important to *be* and not *do*. When
someone says, "I'm feeling very angry, what do I do?" I say,
"Don't do anything, just be. Doing something in such a situation will only make the matter worse. Just experience the
anger and that's it." Just being is also a very powerful form

of meditation and also the easiest to understand. Just be... wherever you are, whatever you are, whatever the situation is, whatever time it is, just observe the moment, be in the moment, live the moment. If we practice just being every moment, our life itself becomes a meditation, similar to a necklace made of beautiful pearls of present moments.

When we become conscious of being, we then really live the present. Our being becomes conscious of itself. Being, consciousness, and life are synonymous. Did you ever think about why we are called human beings—not human doings? That's because our primary objective or purpose is to be, to experience, to live, to be conscious, and not to do or perform. Doing comes later. Since doing involves mind, it creates an illusion of separateness, a continuous conflict within and without. This creates a terrible habit, almost enslavement to constant, never-ending cycles of thinking.

When we identify ourselves with our minds, we actually create a false facade of judgments, definitions, labels, and concepts that actually blocks all our true feelings. It creates a separation between all our true relationships whether between me and myself, me and my close ones, me and nature, me, and the universe. Our minds create the illusion of separation between us and others, completely disregarding the fact that at deeper levels of existence we are all one with the other.

CATCH THE WATCHER

Whenever we try to observe our thoughts for any length of time, we will find that there is someone watching or talking to us. This is a spontaneous process that continually keeps happening in our minds, a continuous form of conversation or discourse. Most importantly, we don't realize that we can stop this process and go into that stillness or peace deep within us. This someone, or the voice, judges or interprets the situations we are at most often either by imagining negative outcomes (anticipating future giving rise to anxiety) or in terms of past events (falling into a negative judgment trap). What this does, in fact, is drain us completely and most often becomes the cause of our physical diseases.

However, we have the ability to come out of this process and save ourselves. As soon as we start observing our own thoughts as a third person, we are in present moment. We must pay attention to those repetitive thought patterns that are causing us untold misery, without being judgmental or condemning. Just watch. This makes us a witness of the events, feelings, thoughts, and emotions and frees us from the bondage of attachment with the same.

The best way to do this is to "Catch the Watcher." Try to catch the one inside us who is watching our thoughts. Then catch this catcher, and so on. Ultimately we find ourselves very deep in the subconscious and actually come out of the negative thought patterns. We can actually feel our deeper self in doing so. We will realize that the power of those impulsive thoughts on us has actually reduced and we will no more identify ourselves with them. This will also open up something beautiful within us—the state of "no thought," a gap between thoughts.

Initially this gap may be small, but slowly you will find that they become extended. This happens once you start experiencing this more often. This is the time when we naturally start living in the present moment. This also becomes a naturally meditative state where we experience deep peace and stillness. However, this should not be confused with lack of alertness. In fact, we are more alert or more fully present during these times as we feel full of life and energy. This way we can actually practice separating ourselves from the mind. It's also fun—try it and see!

SILENCE AND GRATITUDE

"Silence is golden" goes an old proverb, the origin of which is obscured by the mist of time. When we focus on the silence outside us, we can find the silence or stillness within. If we pay more attention to the silence around us than the sounds, we will realize that all the sounds come out of silence and go back into silence. Silence is the beginning and the end. Silence allows the sound to be.

Silence is an opportunity to rest deeply and to truly investigate the vast simplicity at the core of our being. Silence is the peaceful place where we can find the wholeness of our true nature. Excusing ourselves from everyday activities and going into silence from time to time is a great exercise in the present moment awareness. That is when we can allow each experience to flow through us. It is a way to notice our abundance or goodness in others. We can apply this perspective in everyday life to experience life in the *now*.

GRATITUDE

Gratitude is an important virtue that helps us live in each moment happily and to be present in every moment. A well-known saying goes, "I was sad that I had no shoes until I saw a man who had no feet." If we are grateful for each and every small thing, life itself becomes a beautiful journey. Saying "Thank you" every morning for the things that we have in life gives us immense energy to cruise through the challenges of the day. Feeling grateful brings our focus to the present moment.

AT A GLANCE

• The past and the future are illusions.

• The present moment is what life is all about.

• Your first job is being in the moment or experiencing the moment.

• Observing your breathing is the best way to be in the present moment.

CHAPTER 2

DISCOVER YOUR PURPOSE

I want to know, what is my role,
Am I just a part or I am the whole?
I want to know the larger plan of the universe,
Discover where I fit in and find my life purpose.

BE PASSIONATE ABOUT YOUR PURPOSE

When I changed my career to a full time life coach and healer at the age of 40, many eyebrows were raised. After all, anyone who is in an enviable position like I was in my career is not expected to give it all up at that age. Being a mechanical engineer with seventeen years of experience in reputable national and international conglomerates, I had risen to this position through sheer dedication and hard work. Hence, no one initially approved of my decision to plunge into a new career at this stage in my life. They thought I had gone crazy!

A lot of unsolicited advice came my way. Some out of concern, some out of fear, yet others out of sheer ignorance. I realized that every person operated out of his own space, his deep-rooted conditioning, and his own experiences. To the majority, it was a foolish decision to make a career change at this age—and into a field that I was not qualified. Many dissuaded me from walking the path by highlighting the pitfalls, while a few just decided to wait and watch the situation, deliberately avoiding talking about it. This is exactly how the human mind works. If we fail while taking risks in life, we form the belief that "People should not take risks in life." It's like if someone doesn't understand stocks, they advise others never to invest in stocks, and so on.

I get scared when I hear people giving advice to children about their future career and life. Our neighbor once told us, "My nephew is a champion in chess at the national level, but now I have advised him to stop playing chess and focus on his studies, because all that matters in life is how high he scores on his exams."

I was flabbergasted! What a prejudiced view about qualifications! Maybe that gentleman should have thought that perhaps the child is here on earth to excel in chess. But because of advice from someone his family respects, the child did quit playing chess. I came to know later that the child was unable to focus on his studies.

The uncalled-for advice I received did not really bother me much. Deep down in my inner consciousness I knew that I had found my inner calling—my purpose in life—to heal people out of their traumas and to help them discover their true selves.

Although it took me ten long years to accept and acknowledge it, I had firmly decided to follow it now with deep conviction and passion, irrespective of any obstacles or hurdles, whatsoever. I knew that overcoming these roadblocks was the only way to shorten the distance between my life's purpose and me.

PURPOSE OF LIFE—WHAT IS IT?

Many times we are so caught up in the dos and don'ts of life that we turn a deaf ear to our inner voice and disregard our inner feelings. However, deep within, each person knows his or her true purpose in life. It is a "knowing" that comes from within. We just need to be aware and pay attention to it. As we grow up, we comfortably slide into the fixed patterns laid by our parents and society.

THOUGHTS

_____

_____

_____

We are conditioned to believe that certain things are right and certain things are not. We form our own constitution of life based on the way other people want us to live and their experiences and beliefs. We completely forget what we truly want from our own life. In the bargain, we forget our true potential and lose the passion to excel.

WHEN DO WE KNOW?

The process is so designed that we remember our purpose only till we are about two or three years of age, or till we start forming complete sentences when we start talking. Child prodigies such as Wolfgang Mozart, Pablo Picasso, and Shirley Temple are a few of the many known personalities who exhibited their extraordinary talent and passion at a very young age. These people could connect to their purpose at an early age and then follow it. However, as we grow up, slowly our memories start fading. We get trapped in layers of conditioning. That "knowing" gets buried deep inside us, till we realize that we are not happy the way we are living our lives.

We continue feeling a vacuum in life that needs to be filled, but never try to give enough thought and time to that feeling. We feel disconnected from our inner self, our inner core, our inner being. Because of the disconnection from the inner self, most often we start seeking real happiness in external gratification. We want to buy a car, house, get married, and earn wealth, etc., thinking that these things will give us real happiness in life.

There is absolutely nothing wrong in seeking or acquiring material possessions. Each of us has the right to live life in all the comfort and luxuries that we can earn. The actual problem arises when we identify happiness with these and become slaves to our desires. The list of our desires then becomes endless. One desire leads to another and each gets bigger and bigger. In the process, we also fall prey to the competition and comparison of these things with our peers, friends, and neighbors.

We thus fall into a vicious cycle that only causes pain and a tremendous amount of stress. It is only when our body starts giving us signals that we realize that all these years our desires were getting fulfilled at the cost of our health. We still carry on with fulfilling our long wish list, thinking that one day we will be truly happy and satisfied. Only when our body stops supporting us, do we wake up as if from deep sleep.

QUESTIONS AND ANSWERS

Our body is in total despair by then, attacked by all the modern, so-called "lifestyle diseases." We find ourselves confronted with questions such as, "Am I really happy?" "Is this what I wanted from life?" and funnily enough the answer to all these questions is a big "NO."

Soon we realize that despite having a great job, luxuries, and a loving and caring family, we still feel discontented and unhappy. We start questioning life itself: Why are we living? Why do we have to go through all the challenges in life? Why can't life be the same for everybody? Why is there so much disparity in the world? Why am I not happy? However, at our deepest level, our real questions are: Why am I here? What is my purpose?

This is exactly where the quest to find our "true purpose" starts. And when we find our true purpose, all the "whys" are replaced by "hows." That is the time when we really start living, "adding life to our years and not simply years to our life," as it is commonly said. It is never too late to realize this fact. Anytime in life is a good time to start. Once we realize our purpose, it becomes our prime responsibility to take corrective steps in the right direction.

The purpose of life is different for each person. It could be:

- Developing certain virtues such as kindness, patience, courage, honesty, truthfulness, love, surrender, trust, service to others.

- Learning to handle negative emotions such as fear, hatred, anger, pessimism, need for control, revenge, blaming others for failures.

- To develop an attitude of forgiveness or gratitude.

- To learn a certain form of art.

- Serving people or even learning to be served.

- Developing relationships.

- Overcoming a challenge in the form of a physical disability, extreme scarcity or financial burden, addiction (drugs, alcohol, etc.), bad relationships, social status or class, upbringing, unusual circumstances (parental divorce, molestation or rape, etc.).

- Earning name, fame or money.

- Learn to give unconditional love.

- To spread happiness, knowledge, or awareness.

The purpose of life is different and unique for each of us. It is beautifully woven into the script of our lives. We do know our purpose deep within us. We just need to calm ourselves to listen to our inner voice. When we are silent and calm from within, our life's purpose is slowly revealed to us.

CHANGING COURSES

Many times there are repetitive patterns in life or certain road-blocks that are indications that we need to change our course. There could be a deep learning or wisdom coming from a particular repetitive event. Sometimes we may even need to make a U-turn. If even after repeated indications we don't learn or change our path, the universe puts us in a place where we are left with no choice. These are the moments when our true purpose may be revealing itself. We seem to be so trapped in the invisible cage of conditioning and dogmas that we forget life is all about freedom.

It is an irony that although we know that death is the eternal truth. Paulo Coelho once wrote something to this effect "we live as if we are never going to die; and die as if we have never lived." Many times it is our encounter with death that ignites our will to live life to its fullest potential. I have seen this happen with people who have had near-death experiences (NDE).

KIM'S STORY

Kim was a happy-go-lucky person who owned a successful garment export business and enjoyed an enviable status in society. She would always show off her new assets such as her Bentley convertible, the penthouse apartment she bought in a posh locality, and her diamond necklace gifted by her husband on her 40th birthday. She was completely immersed in the material world and sought every opportunity to proudly display her material possessions. Until one day when she was admitted to a hospital for a surgery.

While on operating table under the influence of anesthesia, she suddenly found herself floating near the ceiling. She realized she could see her body lying on the table while doctors were desperately trying to revive her. It dawned on her that she is probably dead, and then she started frantically trying to get back inside her body. At one point, she blacked out and woke up after a day, alive and on the mend.

After a few days, Kim was discharged from the hospital. She didn't know whether what she saw during her operation was a hallucination or not, as no one mentioned it. A few weeks later, she came to know that this incident actually happened, through one of her close friends who knew the doctor present during the operation. She realized that she indeed was clinically dead for a few moments on the operating table!

The near-death experience made such an impact on Kim that she is a completely different person now. She came to understand that the material pleasures never last and started to search for the deeper purpose of her existence on earth. She started a charity organization to help poor and underprivileged people. She also started teaching destitute children and visits senior-care homes to help elderly people.

DEATH AS A REMINDER

I vividly remember attending the funeral of one of my close relatives about ten years back. It was a sudden death and everyone was deeply grieved. During the cremation, I started an internal dialogue within myself. It was as if I was actually face to face with death. It was like a volcano of thoughts and feelings erupting out of my mind. I was restless. "Oh! Even I am going to die one day! Then, why am I here? Am I going to just live in vain and die, or is there a purpose for my being here? Who am I? What happens to me after death? What would people say about me when I am no more?" These questions would not leave me alone.

Sometimes extreme moments of sadness open a doorway to our purpose in life. Especially in the face of death, all external desires, expectations, ego, and fears just fall away like worn-out clothes, leaving only what is truly important—our true selves. We realize that there is absolutely no reason not to follow our hearts.

I could feel my deeper self trying to break free from a cage. *I don't want to live an ordinary life,* I said to myself. This incident led me to search for the deeper meaning of life and its purpose.

PURPOSE AND PASSION

Often we find a call for our passion either by choice or accident. There comes a time in everyone's life, at least once if not more, when we feel, "I wish I could do only this throughout my life." For instance, people who go hiking and explore the mountains wonder if they can continue doing that for the rest of their lives, or when we indulge in something creative such as painting and completely lose track of time, or while singing we experience that inner bliss. These are the real signs that show the way toward our purpose.

When I started on the path of self-discovery, every time I entered a bookshop I was drawn toward the self-help section and would end up buying only those books. About 90 percent of the books in my library are self-help books. I realized that while I was with a group of friends, our conversation would slowly drift in the direction of healing-of-life issues. I was obsessed with this subject and thought about it constantly. I realized that this was something very close to my heart, I had found my passion. I had found my inner calling and wanted to follow my heart without any compromise.

If you find something you are really very passionate about, it often leads to your purpose. Once that happens, you won't have any excuse. You will simply do it, whatever it takes. When you start on the path to your life's purpose, you will be completely at peace with your inner self. You will simply "know" that you have found your purpose.

When we are on the path to our purpose, we are helped by the universe in every possible way to reach our goal. Once we know our purpose, we will find a lot of synchronicities taking place in our lives. We suddenly come across the right books and attract certain people and situations in our lives.

THE PROBLEM WITH DUALITY

We live in the world of duality. We look at everything around us as one or the other. For example, things are either good or bad. We believe in darkness or light, cold or heat, black or white, negative or positive, wrong or right. We judge every event, person, situation, or experience in our lives in the same way, either good or bad. However, when we are working toward our purpose, this concept of either/or does not seem to work. At a higher level of consciousness—from where we operate when we are working toward our purpose—everything that happens or does not happen has a reason behind it.

We understand that darkness is nothing but the absence of light, cold is nothing but the absence of heat, black is the absence of any color, while white is the presence of all colors, whatever looks negative is actually lack of positive, and nothing is wrong as everything is right. Only because we live in the world full of dualities do we go through a life of suffering. Our suffering comes out of ignorance of this basic fact that we are in the universe that is always supportive, guiding us toward the purpose.

THE BIG PICTURE

We automatically get pulled toward something that takes us to our purpose. We often get a déjà vu experience. Since I was a child, I had visions of talking in front of a huge crowd at a stadium, guiding people into meditation. Somehow I knew from within that this is what I am supposed to do. When the time came, my life took a beautiful turn and I met a few wonderful souls on the way, including a few who I hardly knew, who went out of their way to help me follow my purpose in life. This was one sign for me that my life was going on the right track.

The universe works on a larger purpose. You can isolate a drop of water, but when the drop is from an ocean it is part of the whole. This drop cannot be seen as separate from the ocean. Similarly, we are also a part of the humanity altogether. We are part of the whole. The universe does not see us as different from itself; it sees us as its own part. Our individual purpose is in fact magnificently integrated into the purpose of the universe.

The life of every human being has a larger meaning, which is why it becomes even more important for us to know it and work toward it. We just need to trust the process, and not judge it from our limited perspective. Our higher self always knows and will always guide us toward our purpose. What we think is wrong at a given point in time, may be good for us in the larger plan.

AT A GLANCE

- You come with a purpose to be fulfilled in this lifetime.

- The purpose of life is different and unique for each person.

- You are helped by the universe in all possible ways to reach your purpose.

- Your higher self always knows and will always guide you toward your purpose.

CHAPTER 3

CHOICE IS YOUR BIRTHRIGHT—EXERCISE IT

Every moment is a crossroad, and I have the choice
To move toward my purpose and listen to the inner voice.
I can choose my path to greatness and life goal;
Making the right choice, gives satisfaction to my soul.

Ionce heard an interesting fable about a man who paid a heavy price for the choice he made. On a winter day, he went to hike up a mountain. Due to bad weather, he was not able to get back to the base camp at the foot of the mountain. As night approached, the weather became worse. The harsh, cold winds and the darkness of the night made it difficult for the man to climb down. As he was descending, he stumbled and rolled down the mountain. Afraid that he would surely die, he started screaming for help as he fell.

Suddenly as he was tumbling down a cliff, his hands touched something that felt like a branch and he grabbed it. He felt relieved when he realized he had come to a halt. He started shouting for help with the hope that someone would hear him and come to his rescue. There was no response and to make matters worse it was a pitch dark winter night, so he could not see a thing around him.

He became tired of hanging in the air and felt that he would die soon. He started praying, "Please help me, God, please save me, I don't want to die, I want to live." To his great astonishment, he heard a soothing voice that said, "My dear child, I will save you, just let go of what you are holding and you will be saved."

The man thought his mind was playing tricks on him and was hearing voices. Again the voice said, "Son, do not delay, just have faith and let go, you will be saved." The man told himself, *Don't let go...hold on tight...your mind is playing tricks. If you let go you will die. Don't listen to the voice.*

The next morning, when the villagers came out of their homes, they saw a man hanging from a tree just a few feet above the ground. He was frozen and dead. The villagers were talking among themselves, "Poor man, why didn't he jump to the ground. He could have easily found a house and taken shelter. He could have lived!"

* * *

The journey of life is like climbing a mountain. The destination is the peak. Each of us is born to reach the top and has all the potential to do so. But as we climb, there are many forces that pull us back; these are in the form of distractions, emotions, ego, desires, fears, doubts, etc. At each step we have a choice, whether to let ourselves be pulled back by these forces or march ahead. The higher we go, the stronger these forces become; hence, the greater the agony when we fall down.

Choice is our birthright, and we must exercise it. The choice we make at every moment during the journey determines our speed and the time we take to reach the peak—our ultimate goal, our purpose in life. We are all born on this planet with a purpose, to be lived during this lifetime. We may have set certain goals for ourselves to reach or achieve during the life span. Once we have decided what we want to achieve or where we want to reach, we set on the path toward it.

FREE WILL

As human beings we have been bestowed upon with a wonderful gift—free will—intellect along with the power to choose. Having discovered our purpose, choice plays an extremely crucial role in finding the right path. It is our choice that either takes us toward our purpose or away from it. Our life graph is marked with tiny dots of the choices we make at every given moment; and each moment is a crossroad. At every moment, we have a choice to move toward our goal or away from it. A series of such choices marks our path, which when analyzed show the direction in which our life is moving. There is always a choice and free will to change our direction at each moment, if we find we are going away from our purpose or goals.

There is another dimension that plays a vital role in the choice-making process. This is the inner feeling or guidance that comes from the "knowing" or from our hearts. It is commonly said, "When you are stuck while making a choice, listen to your heart. The heart is always right." Our heart knows exactly what is right for us.

CHOICES

The choices we make are often labeled as right or wrong, depending on the consequences. For example, a heavy smoker has been advised not to smoke due to ill health. The next time somebody offers the person a cigarette, he has a choice to make. If he accepts the smoke, he falls prey to his desires and hence further deteriorates his health. If he refuses, he develops courage and strength, and gives himself a chance to live a healthy life.

However, there is no right or wrong in absolute terms. We can define this in a different way though. Any choice that is in sync with our goal or purpose and takes us toward it is right for us. Similarly, any choice that is not in sync or not favorable to our goal or purpose and takes us away from it is wrong for us. The whole system of free will is so designed that even if we make a choice that is not in sync with our purpose in the present moment, the very next moment is our next chance to correct ourselves. But the most important point of choice is the *now*. The gateway to our highest potential and the highest possibilities is only in the *now*.

THE DOMINO EFFECT

Merriam-Webster's Dictionary says that the domino effect is a simple chain reaction that occurs when a small change causes a similar change nearby, which then will cause another similar change, and so on in linear sequence, by analogy to a falling row of dominoes standing on end. The domino effect also relates to a chain of events.

Let us say you have an important presentation to make early in the morning for a big client in the office. You forget to set the alarm and frantically wake up to realize that you are terribly late. In haste while shaving, you cut yourself. Looking at your cut, your wife lovingly offers to apply antiseptic lotion, but you simply yell at her as you are agitated. Your wife gets upset and in a foul mood goes to wake up the kids, scolding them for sleeping late. The kids, not knowing the situation, wake up in a grumpy mood, crying.

During all the chaos, you somehow manage to get ready and walk out the door. You get into your car and while backing out, you hit your neighbor's car. Hearing the noise, the neighbor comes out and enters into an argument with you. By now you have not only lost valuable time but are on the verge of losing your mind too. You drive fast, and because you are already late and anxious, you drive through a red signal only to be stopped by the traffic police. You argue but finally pay the fine and move ahead.

After reaching the office, your anxiety increases when you see your colleagues and the client already seated in the conference room waiting for you. You feel embarrassed and guilty. Consequently, the presentation does not go well and you lose an important contract. You call your subordinate and fire him, putting the blame on him for improper inputs in the presentation. At the end of the day you are filled with remorse, guilt, and anger. Finally you label the day as a "bad day."

GOOD DAYS AND BAD DAYS

But the truth is—there are no bad days. It's the choices we make that result in a good or bad day for us. In this example, at every juncture you had the free will to choose your reaction to each situation. Although you got up late, you had a choice between getting anxious or remaining calm. When your wife offered to apply lotion you had a choice to operate out of love instead of anger. When your neighbor started arguing with you, you had a choice to politely admit the mistake and say, "Sorry." This would have helped in keeping your anger in control. While driving to the office, you had a choice to drive at a slower speed and not drive through the red signal. When you arrived late at office you had a choice to feel guilty and angry or to accept it and apologize for being late. One choice always leads to another, and every time you had a choice to correct the previous one, by choosing differently. Thus the domino effect could have been completely avoided.

THOUGHTS

_____

_____

_____

Now imagine the gravity of this domino effect on your life. If you call a day full of wrong choices a bad day, what will you call a life full of wrong choices, a bad life? Life beautifully presents us with an opportunity at every moment to correct the past wrong choices. Exercising the right choice means taking responsibility of the wrong ones and correcting them in the very next moment.

Suppose you are driving from one city to another and you arrive at a Y junction, the road ahead splits into two and there are no signs to guide you. You take one of the two roads and after driving a bit you realize that you are on the wrong road. What will you do now? You can either make a U-turn, returning to the point where you made a choice and take the other road; or you can find the nearest road that connects to the road that leads to your destination. In life, however, we cannot make a U-turn and come back to the point of choice. We have to make corrections from wherever we are and find the path taking us back on the road to our goal or purpose.

TO LIVE BY CHOICE OR BY CHANCE

While driving we are very cautious and make sure we take the correct road that leads to our destination. So why can't we be even more cautious when making choices that lead us toward our purpose, the ultimate goal?

We always have a choice. Our reaction to the situations in our life is our free-will. Many times, we just step back and allow life to happen to us rather than taking life in our hands. We blame our destiny instead of creating our destiny. We live by chance and not by choice. All the great achievers or the people who have lived their purpose have always lived by choice and not by chance. By making the right choices they opened the gateways that helped them reach their goals. They always focused on their goals and made choices that took them further. Thus they also created their own destiny.

TO MAKE CHANGES OR FIND EXCUSES

Finding excuses is always an easy way out, but not the right choice to make. Many face this decision on a daily basis. For example, we choose to lose our excess body weight as we realize it's a threat to our health and, of course, our public image. We decide to make a change—the right choice. We understand the gravity of the situation and after all, no one wants to fall sick. So we enroll ourselves in a gym for a year after a lot of deliberation, and decide to follow a strict diet plan.

Everything goes well for the first few weeks—or even just a few days. Slowly lethargy sets in and we come up with amazing and creative excuses for not going to the gym such as, "Work is more important, I can definitely skip the gym," or "I'm very tired today, I must rest," and so on. Eventually we also start eating junk food giving the excuse, "I'll just have a couple today, after all I should enjoy each and every moment." And so we start off on a spree of making excuses—making the wrong choices. We are conditioned to take the path of least resistance, which ultimately proves to be our bane.

TO BE MANIPULATED OR MOTIVATED

When I chose to follow my purpose, some of my friends thought that it was their moral duty to point out all the pitfalls in the career I had chosen. One of them very bluntly said, "This is not your cup of tea. I don't think you will succeed in this. You are better off in your job." When this came from the person I adored and respected, I was disheartened. I began to lose focus on my goal and allowed self-doubt to sink in.

However, I knew deep within that I was on the right path. After spending a few days in dejection, I realized that I had a choice to either to be dejected or to be motivated. I chose to be motivated. I told myself, "I take complete responsibility for my life choices and the consequences thereafter. If someone tries to deviate me from this path, I will spring forward with double the zest. I choose to be motivated to excel and not to be disheartened by anyone's perspective about my life choices." And here I am writing this book, a result of the choice I made at that point in life.

TO EXCEL OR TO COMPETE

We live in a world of competition. Most will experience competitions at each stage of life. When a toddler goes to kindergarten there is competition for admission, as the child grows there is competition in school, after studies to get a job we go through intense competition, and then in the job there is competition to succeed. We cannot get away from competition struggles until the very end of life.

Even to be termed as successful in the eyes of society, we have to compete; as success in people's eyes is all about how much material wealth someone gathers. In the process, we end up in an endless, self-defeating, or pointless pursuit of either peers' adulation or approval of others around us. This pursuit could even be to attract the attention of people around us, our friends, colleagues, relatives, sometimes even parents, as gaining attention seems to make us feel important in their eyes.

Eventually we become slaves to competition. As is commonly said, "The trouble with the rat race is that even if you win, you're still a rat." We work hard to be one step higher than others, which gives rise to bloated egos. Unknowingly, and sometimes knowingly, we try to prove ourselves superior to others. However, the problem with this whole system of competition is that although we are trying to be or do better than another, there is no effort to excel. We fail to excel because we are working only toward the standards set by somebody else. This competition induces a lot of stress and also drains our energy levels.

We all have enormous potential within us from the time of our birth—every person, without exception. This potential, which can be used to reach excellence in whatever field we are in, is wasted when we compete against each other. While competing, the whole focus is on being better than the other and not on exceling. In order to excel, we need to set our own standards and milestones and work toward achieving them. We always have a choice to excel or to compete. If we choose to excel, we come out of the fray—rat race—and free ourselves from the bondage of competition.

ANGER OR LOVE

When we operate out of anger, we build walls; when we operate out of love, we build bridges. We always have a choice, to operate out of anger or love in any given situation.

Kapil is a doctor who works in a famous hospital in Mumbai. Every time we met, I always found him frustrated and full of anger. He said it was work pressure getting too much for him. One day he went home early from the hospital because he had a severe migraine headache. He was resting in his room when suddenly his 10-year-old son burst in, ecstatic and shouting at the top of his voice. "Yes! I made it!" he said. "Dad, I got selected for my school cricket team!" and started dancing.

Kapil was already in a foul mood because of the bad headache. He got enraged and snapped at his child, "What's there to get so excited about? Don't scream like that—go to your room." Feeling dejected, the boy entered his room and slammed the door behind him. This incident affected him so much that he stopped playing cricket. I heard later that when Kapil came to know about this, he felt extremely guilty and could not forgive himself. Operating out of anger always leads to guilt and regret, and sometimes the damage is irreversible. We must stay away from anger, as the only person who gets hurt the most is us. The choice is ours.

FEAR OR COURAGE

Courage is an extremely important ingredient of a successful life. "Everything you want is on the other side of fear" and "Your greatest treasures lie beyond your greatest fears" are common sayings, which are so very true. Courage is not just physical bravery. Courage ranges from physical strength and endurance to mental stamina and innovation.

Fear is a negative emotion that acts as an iron wall to our progress, and to overcome this wall we need courage. Fear has the capacity to completely destroy a person, whereas courage has the power to pull someone out of the worst situation. We must choose to have the courage to be honest and truthful, to ourselves and others, to do the right thing in life, to take responsibility for our actions.

We must have the courage to say no when we have to. We must be courageous to ask for what is rightfully ours. Choosing courage to accept certain truths about us, without being fearful about the consequences, is a great way to live successfully.

TO HAVE FAITH OR DOUBT

Faith fills us with peace, serenity, and understanding, while doubt inflicts us with frustration, anger, remorse. Faith opens many doorways to reach our purpose, while doubt always pulls us back. The choice is ours, whether to operate out of faith or doubt.

SELF-ESTEEM OR SELF-PITY

Suppose your boss in a fit of anger says, "You are good for nothing; you mess up everything you do." Here you have a choice to either take offense and indulge in self-pity thinking you are really a mess, or to tell yourself, *I know I am the best at what I do, the boss must be in a foul mood today.* This applies to every situation. We often fall prey to self-pity and low self-esteem. This eventually pulls us down and takes us away from the path of our highest potential. The choice lies with us whether to take these situations or comments seriously or just let them go and believe in our true worth.

TO FORGIVE OR TO BLAME

Blaming someone does not take us anywhere. If someone hurls an abuse at you, you have the choice to take it or leave it. Nobody can hurt you unless you allow them to do so. Forgiveness is a practice that takes us up the ladder and above the person who has hurt us. When somebody hurts us, we always have a choice, either to forgive that person or blame the person. Everything has to do with you, not the other person or situation.

During my corporate years, one of my subordinates created serious misunderstandings between me and my immediate boss. This strained our relationship, which was otherwise very friendly. Once I found out the real culprit of the rumors was the subordinate, I angrily confronted him and he accepted his mistake and apologized for it.

But it was not possible for me to forgive him. I was feeling the hurt and betrayal continuously in the next days, and as I became more affected, my productivity decreased. This unforgiving attitude eventually affected my health adversely, while he was leading a happy life. Finally after a couple of weeks, I let go of the hurt and completely forgave him. That's when I experienced peace.

ACCEPTANCE OR RESISTANCE

Sometimes it is good to accept the things we cannot change and move on in life. The more we resist something, the more severe the issue grows to be. Resistance also causes friction and a considerable loss of energy and prevents us from moving toward our goals.

A gentleman brought his son to me for healing. The son, ever since his childhood, wished to become an artist, but his father had forced his son to study engineering. I later came to know that becoming an engineer was the father's own unaccomplished desire. The son had gone into severe depression and had developed several physical ailments for giving up his dream of being an artist and doing something he never liked.

Finally, the son gave up everything, including his studies. Had the father accepted what his son wanted to do, things would have been completely different. Because the father chose to resist his son's wishes and forced his expectation on him, it resulted in the son choosing to go against the wishes of his father and stop doing anything at all. Eventually the whole family was in despair.

Remember, by exercising our choice we are creating our future. And by making the right choices we are moving toward our purpose or goals one step at a time, every moment. *We are always where we choose to be.*

AT A GLANCE

- When you know your goal, you must choose your path.

- Choice is your birthright, and you must exercise it.

- Trust your heart—it knows exactly what is right for you.

- Be courageous to ask for what is rightfully yours.

CHAPTER 4

JUST DO IT—NOW

I know my goal, my life's destination,
My purpose, my chosen path, my vocation.
I have to take the first step on my stride;
Only when I dare, luck 'll be on my side.

The little baby eagle watched with awe as its mother flew fearlessly high up in the sky. It knew that it is also meant to fly. After the initial struggle, the day finally arrived when the young eagle was ready to soar high in the sky. Without any fear or hesitancy, the eagle took off with pride, never looking back.

* * *

In a little village, surrounded by beautiful mountains and lakes, lived a boy. Every day on his way to school he would pass by a lake and watch other little boys dive into the lake from the top of a hillock. For the little boy, this was a daring and heroic act that he was eager to try, but could not. His mother had strictly warned him against trying this stunt, as she thought it was too dangerous and could prove fatal. This warning was enough to scare the boy and he never tried the stunt. But every day he passed by the lake, he secretly wished to try. However, he never attempted it.

After many years had passed, an old man was narrating his childhood stories to his grandson, sitting near the same lake. Suddenly his grandson said, "Grandpa, let's take a dip in the lake. We'll go to the top of that hillock and jump from there."

The old man immediately reacted by telling the little boy how risky it was to try this stunt, but the boy replied with all enthusiasm, "Oh come on, Grandpa, it will be fun! Don't be afraid, I'm with you." Saying so, his grandson pulled the unwilling grandfather by the hand and took him uphill. Looking down at the lake from the hilltop, the old man remembered how his mother had scared him about this little stunt.

He then told the story to his grandson. The grandson said, "Well, Grandpa, it's not that high, it will be okay. Just see how I do it and follow me. You have nothing to be afraid of." The boy then jumped into the lake and called out to the old man, "Come on, Grandpa, just do it! Don't think too much and don't waste time. You've been waiting all your life to do this, this is your chance...don't lose it!"

As he stood there, the old man thought of all the years of his life that had passed by. He had wasted so much time, but thanks to his grandson, now was the moment he could finally try the feat. He took a deep breath, looked down at his cheering grandson and said to himself, *Just do it.*

And the old man jumped into the lake. When he surfaced from the water, he was laughing like a little boy and his grandson was clapping for him. "You did it, Grandpa, you did it!" he said jubilantly.

The old man, even as a little boy, knew that it was safe to plunge from the hilltop, as he had seen other boys do. But his mother had *instilled* the fear of consequences in him so he never gathered the courage, even later in his life, to try. Only when his grandson *assured* him that he would be all right did he go ahead without any fear.

The same is true in our lives as well. We tend to avoid doing things simply because we give too much importance to other people's perspectives. We are guided by others' opinions, never actually daring to try things ourselves. We stop ourselves, thinking we will fail or get hurt because that's what people tell us. By doing this we live someone else's version of life, restricting ourselves and following standards set by others, not us.

TAKE THE FIRST STEP

After identifying life's purpose and making the choice to walk on that path, do not waste even a single moment waiting around or mulling over the decision. Just do it! A car is stationary when parked and is only capable of moving when the ignition key is turned. We too are initially in a state of inertia when we first find our purpose, our goal. Kick-start the ignition by taking the first initiative, release the break by lifting the veil of fears, and put your life in gear by self-motivation and determination. Then push the accelerator to start on your journey!

If you stay too long in the state of inertia, there is a high possibility that you may never take off on the path toward your goals. When we have just found our highest goal in life, we are like young saplings that require nurturing. There are many dangers lurking around such as fear, doubt, and unsolicited advice to wither us. The only way to survive is to overcome these dangers by holding on to our inner strength and having faith in our abilities.

THOUGHTS

_____

_____

_____

Fast forward twenty years into your life. Then look back and ask yourself, how do you feel? If you are feeling happy about the decisions you took, that's great! But if you feel regret for not having pursued your chosen goals, then you have all the reasons to just do it—now. By not doing so, you are running the risk of not living your life completely.

IMRAN'S TALE

A few years back, my friend, Imran, got his driving license and was very excited to drive around by himself. It gave him the feeling of being in control. However, his father would always caution him saying, "Be careful," "Drive a little slower," "Avoid the highways right now," "Since you are new to driving, don't drive every day." Frustrated with all the unsolicited advice, Imran eventually decided to give up driving and now prefers traveling by public transport.

The point is, even when you are well-equipped and ready to take on the journey of life, you will face adversities and roadblocks. Remember, you have chosen your path after adequate deliberation. Believe your inner voice, which will guide you throughout your life. Keep telling yourself, *This is my path, my purpose, my goal, my life. I should not wait any longer. I have made a choice. I must take the first step toward my goal ASAP!*

All great things begin small. Even though the road ahead may not be clear now, you must believe that you are on the right path. Vasco da Gama, the great Portuguese explorer, led a fleet of four ships and a crew of 170 men when he set sail to find India. En route he faced many difficulties, but he finally achieved his goal—he discovered the sea route from Europe to India in 1498.

Had Vasco da Gama sat around thinking and weighing the pros and cons even before setting sail, he would have probably never sailed. But he knew what he wanted to achieve and did not let anything distract him. Our goal should be the central focus of our lives and nothing should be able to pull us away from it.

OVERCOMING NEGATIVE FEELINGS

Many times a strong feeling keeps nudging us to begin our path, but we are either too scared or too lazy to respond. To suppress that feeling, we often engross ourselves in our daily routine. We sideline those feelings and thoughts, and continue living our lives as if they do not matter. However, in the process, we risk never finding out what would have happened if only we had listened to our inner voice.

It is very important to ask ourselves how we feel from within at the thought of pursuing our calling. Our inner strength will always guide and help us take that first step. We must not stop exploring new ideas and opportunities. Our natural human fears of failure, embarrassment, being judged, or change may try to stop us from trying new things. But it is our prime responsibility to rise above these fears.

A successful and deeply joyous life, ultimately, is a collection of small and unique experiences. The more unique experiences you have, the more interesting your life will become. Hence, it is imperative to seek opportunities to have as many new experiences as possible. You must also make sure that you share these with the people you care about.

When I first thought of writing this book, I did not ponder much on whether it would sell or not, whether people would appreciate it or not. I just wanted to share my life's experiences with everyone, connect to people, reach out to them, and help them discover their purpose in life. From that first thought to the time I actually started writing the book, there were many challenges and hurdles that I faced. But soon I realized that this was not just any passing thought, it was an inner calling, because each time I ignored the voice that urged me to write, I felt restless and disturbed. So I listened to my inner voice and started writing.

I realized that the challenges and hurdles I faced earlier were my own fears and self-doubts trying to stop me from pursuing my passion. And when I tackled them with courage, they just disappeared. I had very little professional writing skills, but I believed in myself. I also kept complete faith on the universe to guide me at every step of the way. I knew that writing this book would take me closer to my life's goals. Each time I sat to write, I felt extremely happy and blissful. Once I made up my mind, I did not allow anything to discourage or distract me.

Humans are gifted with a wonderful faculty, the intellect, which helps us choose and make decisions. But there's a big difference between knowing what to do and actually doing it. Knowledge is completely useless without action. The problem arises when we are too scared or skeptical to take the first step. Understand that no one in the whole world can guarantee what's going to happen in the next moment. This moment is all you have. You can decide only in this moment to take that step toward what you long to do. We discover the real joy when we start walking the chosen path. Nothing comes easy in life, but when we make up our minds to just do it, then we have to take the first step. There may be tough times, even discouragements, but nothing should deter us from taking that first important step.

MISTAKES ARE GOLDEN

The advantage of living in our comfort zone is that we never have to take any risks. The disadvantage is that we will never know how life would have turned out had we come out of our comfort zone and taken a risk. It is okay to make mistakes. As a matter of fact it is great, as mistakes happen only when there is action—when we are doing something or taking steps. It is a sure indication that we are not still or stagnant, that we are actually trying to succeed. Remember, what stagnates, eventually rots and stinks!

Mistakes are also great teachers, as they teach us important lessons. We cannot expect to be perfect unless we make mistakes, correct ourselves, and learn from the experience. In life, it is all about taking chances, and never about getting chances. Opportunities need to be created. Yes, the outcome cannot be guaranteed, but until you try, how you find out? It is better to try and fail and try again, than never to try at all.

DON'T MISS THE OPPORTUNITY

I happened to read a story while surfing the Internet once. The source of the story is unknown but it is worth being shared here. It goes as follows. A young man wished to marry a farmer's beautiful daughter. He approached the farmer to ask for his daughter's hand. The farmer looked at him and said, "I'm going to release three bulls, one at a time. If you can catch the tail of any one of them, you can marry my daughter." The young man agreed to do so and waited for the first bull in the field. The barn door opened and out came the biggest, meanest looking bull he had ever seen. The young man quickly decided that this is definitely not his bull.

So he ran over to the side and let the bull pass through the field and out the gate. The barn door opened again. The young man was stunned to see an even bigger and much more ferocious bull than the first one. The young man said to himself, *I have to wait for the next one if I don't want to die young.* He immediately ran to the side and let the vicious animal pass through the field and go out the back gate.

The barn door opened for the third time. The young man was extremely happy to see a small little creature. This was the skinniest bull he had seen in his life. *This is my bull!* he said to himself with a beaming face. As the tiny bull came toward him, the young man lunged at its back. To his astonishment, this bull had no tail!

There will be opportunities at every corner of our lives. But always keep in mind that they will not wait indefinitely for us. We need to recognize them and then grab them with both hands. Once you let them pass, they are gone forever. Worse, someone else will grab them before you do and you will lose out to another.

We should also strive to cultivate the winning habit of creating unique opportunities for ourselves. Some opportunities are easy to take advantage of, some are difficult. It really doesn't matter. If we get bogged down by circumstances, we will always find excuses. The idea is to live life beyond excuses and live an extraordinary life. Enterprising people will see opportunities in everything they come across. They will keep their eyes and minds open to grab even the smallest opportunity. If something goes wrong, they will not be disturbed, but will find ways to overcome the challenges. They have the courage to see things differently, to go above the crowd.

Sometimes we really want to pursue our goals, but we don't have the resources to pursue them. There is a saying, "When universe guides, it also provides." As odd as it may sound, have complete faith in the universe. When you are on the path of your goals or purpose, it will help with everything that you require, at the right time.

ESCAPE VELOCITY

When we throw an object in the air, gravity pulls it down. The faster you throw it, the higher it goes and the longer it takes to come back to the ground. If you keep increasing the speed, at some point the speed is fast enough for the object to escape the gravitational pull of the earth. When the object is thrown at that speed, it does not come back to the earth. This speed is called "escape velocity" in physics.

How does this relate to our lives? Well, we all experience the gravitational pull while starting something new. Say, for example, I decide to get up early in the morning and go for a run every day from tomorrow onward. I set the alarm for 6 a.m. before I go to sleep. In the morning, I experience the enormous pull of earth's gravity when I am trying to get up at 6 a.m. The bed is like a strong magnet, and I am being dragged toward it as if my body is made of pure iron. I somehow manage to go past the first challenge, get ready, and successfully complete my commitment to myself.

I successfully follow the running schedule. I run for the first three days until I start experiencing fatigue and initial muscle pain because of my lack of exercise for a long time. This really complicates the issue for me, as it feels like now my bed, along with the magnetic pull, also has strong glue applied to it. To top it off, I find the excuse-making part of my mind has started working overtime. I experience excellent, unmatchable excuses coming to me at great speeds. I finally draw the conclusion that I cannot get up with my present resolve and determination. I stop going for the run on the fifth day.

In this example, my resolve is the speed at which I launch myself to fulfill my commitment to myself; in this case, the morning run. The stronger my resolve was, the more days I was able to continue my run. To be consistent in doing this continuously over a long period of time, I really need to have the resolve that will break all barriers. I compare this with escape velocity. Only when I am able to get myself free from the mental and physical obstacles will I be consistent in moving toward my goals with matchless speed.

Constant unswerving efforts and perseverance takes us to that uppermost slot of success in life. If we pursue something with dedication, give it our heart and soul, it becomes a habit. To make a new habit, I encourage you to continue doing the same for at least 15 days, which is how long it takes me. This may change from person to person, but the resolve to continue doing something over a long period has to be cultivated using our willpower and how much we want that habit.

According to Newton's first law of motion, an object in the state of rest continues to remain at rest or an object in the state of motion continues to remain in motion unless and until an external force is applied to it. The rest state is called inertia. In common parlance, we also call it lethargy. Many times it is sheer laziness that stops us from pursuing our inner calling. Lethargy has no cure. Self-motivation or willpower is the only cure to break free from this confinement and leap out.

FEAR OF CHANGE

Change is sometimes extremely difficult and poses a huge hurdle in front of us. We are like a bird that has been living inside a cage for a long time; even if the cage is opened, the bird will not fly away. It has been conditioned to live inside the cage, which is its safety net or its comfort zone. We too become so ensconced in our present environment that it is nearly impossible to pluck us out of that cushy comfort zone.

The only thing that is constant is change. We must welcome change and be open to new challenges and opportunities. We must take a moment and look around and ask ourselves, *Am I really where I'm meant to be?* If the answer is "No," then it's time to fly away and embrace change.

FEAR OF BEING JUDGED

Many times we are too embarrassed to follow our passion because we are afraid of what others will think of us. For example, imagine that you are a young executive working for a big business company. You decide to quit your cushy job and pursue singing as a full-time career. How do you think people around you will react? The answer is simple. Many, including your family and friends, may ridicule you for such a decision. They may even label this as a serious mistake and you as crazy. But just remember one thing, if your heart says this is your true passion and it really makes you happy, then what others say becomes irrelevant. Gather the courage to face the world and just do it!

FEAR OF FAILURE

Be an optimist. It really helps. We must see or visualize ourselves succeeding at whatever we undertake. If we visualize failure, then only failure is what we get. Fear of failure comes as a result of either our past experiences or experiences of others around us. Sometimes we get discouraged by seeing others fail having taken a similar path. We assume that we will fail too. We must always remember that this is our journey and it will have its unique, new enriching experiences. Each of us is here with a unique purpose which we must follow, against all odds. Do not be afraid to walk on your own path, even if it means diverting from the set rules or paradigm or dogmas.

When we want to pursue something new, self-doubt may creep in. Remember, if you feel the inclination, it means you also possess the ability to make it happen. I again recap here that the universe has already made big plans for us and has gifted us the necessary abilities to pursue our goals. The apple seed does not know its potential to produce apples, but the farmer does!

Once there was a man who prayed to God to let him win the lottery. Every day he prayed sincerely, but nothing happened. But he still continued praying. After listening to his prayers for many days, God was frustrated and appeared before the man. God said, "My dear child, I have been listening to your prayers for so long. I want to help you win a lottery. But can you please go and buy a lottery ticket first!"

The problem with many of us is, while in a state of inertia, we expect an external force to magically make us begin or start our path. But that's not how it works. We have to personally take the initial step toward our goal.

Once we have identified our life goals and chosen to pursue them, why let anything stop us now? The more we sit on it, ponder or doubt, the more time we waste and delay the process of completion. Do not allow anything or anyone to discourage or distract your focus. Life is short, yet amazing. Enjoy the ride.

AT A GLANCE

- Once you have chosen your path, you must take the first step.

- Never delay anything—just do it!

- Mistakes are great teachers, so even if you falter, you will learn.

- Believe your inner voice, which will guide you throughout your life.

- A successful and deeply joyous life, ultimately, is a collection of small and unique experiences.

CHAPTER 5

THE UNSTOPPABLE YOU

I will keep moving, come what may,
No challenge or difficulty can block my way.
Not ready to give up, on any day,
Even if I failed before, I'll win today.

REALIZING YOUR HIGHEST POTENTIAL

Like a river I flow, meandering around all the hurdles that try to stop me; making my own way, I move forward fiercely. It is my destiny to reach my goal, to merge with the ocean and I will not be stopped. One day I will merge, overcoming and triumphing over everything that stands in my way—because I'm unstoppable. I know that the only way to reach my destination on time, overcoming all hurdles on my journey, is to ride on wheels that are unstoppable.

* * *

It was October 20, 1968, the final day of Olympic Games being held in Mexico City. On that hot Sunday afternoon, the men's marathon started with 74 participants. Only 57 finished the race. At 7 p.m.—almost an hour after the last runner had crossed the finish line, medals had already been awarded, even the games closing ceremony had already been completed—the announcer asked the remaining guests to stand back from the finish area.

Then a lone runner entered the stadium moving slowly. The audience was amazed at what they saw next. John Stephen Akhwari of Tanzania was covered with blood when he hobbled in. He had fallen down while running and was hurt badly. His knee was dislocated and his head was bleeding. He was asked many times by the authorities to quit the race, but he did not. He fell many times, yet still dragged himself to finish the marathon, limping. The response of the crowd was overwhelming with loud applause and cheers. His body was exhausted and injured, but his determination was not.

When Akhwari was asked the next day why, even after sustaining serious injuries and knowing that he would not win a medal, he continued to the finish line, he replied, "My country did not send me 5,000 miles just to start the race; they sent me 5,000 miles to finish the race." Akhwari could never win an Olympic gold medal, but he became an example of sheer grit and never-give-up spirit. He was unstoppable.

In our lives, once we have found our goals and choose to pursue them, we should be unstoppable. Then no obstacle is too big to overcome. Passion, power, perseverance, and planning should be the four wheels of the vehicle we ride to move forward unplugged.

Like Akhwari, we are all here to finish the race, to excel, and win in our respective fields and life. We may face obstacles on our way such as ill health, financial setbacks, deceit from those we trust, wrong advice, and our own emotional issues—fear, anger, depression, failures, etc. In spite of all that, make it a point to keep on moving at any cost because as soon as you stop, it becomes twice as difficult to start again. Do not let any excuse stop your journey toward your goal.

Let's say that being unstoppable is very much like winning a horse race. The goal is to reach the finish line first and that's all the jockey is thinking about while riding. Have you ever seen the jockey take a break to stretch his arms or allow the horse to wander around? No, of course not. Because the jockey cannot afford to do that if the goal is to win the race. Once you know your goal, set a deadline to achieve it, be focused, maintain consistency, ignore distractions, and transcend the obstacles in your way.

UNSTOPPABLE ARON

Aron Ralston left his job as a mechanical engineer with Intel in Phoenix, Arizona, at the age of 25 in order to pursue a life of climbing mountains. On April 26, 2003, Aron was hiking through a canyon when he experienced a terrible accident. While descending a slot canyon, a suspended boulder dislodged and came down, crushing his right hand and forearm, pinning it against the canyon wall. After five days of horror and left with no choice, he had to break free by cutting his trapped arm. Aron lived to tell his story, which was later adapted to a movie.

Today Aron Ralston draws on the determination that brought him back to continue climbing mountains. The self-amputation of his arm caused an infection in the bone, giving him a 50-50 chance of survival. He thought then, that this was not the life he fought so hard to come back from, to get back to. He vowed to come out as a winner; and from that moment he started getting better. The day after he received his first prosthetic arm, he went rock climbing.

In June 2008, Aron solo climbed Denali, the highest mountain peak in North America (6194 m) and then skied down. He was the first person with a disability to ski down Denali. Aron Ralston did not break down after his injury; rather, he broke the barriers of his thinking. He remained unstoppable. His story inspires many today not because he had to cut off his arm to break free, but because he achieved his life ambitions despite his disability.

A DANCER'S TALE

In 1981, a 16-year-old girl went through a harrowing experience after doctors decided to amputate her leg due to a freak accident and gangrene setting in her right foot. The unfortunate teenager was an expert dancer even at that young age. This incident shook her from inside and threatened to end her passion.

However, she did not give up and refused to accept defeat. After being fitted with an artificial leg, she started to practice dance again. It took her two years of sheer dedication and practice to do her first dance show after the accident. She has not looked back since then. Due to her willpower, hard work, and positive attitude, Sudha Chandran became an acclaimed dancer and an award-winning actor. Her inspirational story was adapted for a highly praised movie. She continues to work in films and television and has never let the past incident limit her way of life.

Adversities in our lives have their own way to impart lessons that make us stronger. People who have undergone severe circumstances in life and have overcome because of their willpower and resolve to succeed. They are real heroes. These people did not let the unfortunate incidents in their lives to get the better of them. This ability to fight back, to keep on moving despite misfortune and hardships, is what makes us unstoppable. Life goes on. So should we. If we stop at any point, worrying about what has happened in life or what might happen, we are losing precious life moments.

SIMPLE MATH

If we take 75 years as an average life span of humans, how many days do we have in our entire life? Exactly 27,375 days. Out of these we lose about 7,375 days growing up. What is left is only about 20,000 days. About 5,000 days of old age will be a waste as we do not have enough energy left to do what we really want. The balance is only 15,000. Just imagine, only 15,000 days in your entire life.

How do you think we should spend these days? Many have spent half of these days doing mundane things. How many would like to just come to this planet and go back without being noticed? No one, right?

The thought I am trying to bring in here is simple. Do you think you are born to live an average life? If your answer is no, then this book is written for you. If you really think that you are here to excel, to be a winner, to do better than what others expect you to do—live your life successfully—then I am sure you can draw a lot from this book.

Becoming the best and being unstoppable are basically mental approaches. We become as we think. If we think of greatness, our lives will turn toward greatness. If we think of not looking back and moving ahead in life, beyond our limitations, the universe will help us in doing just that.

MIND MATTERS

To be unstoppable, it is essential to practice discipline and control over the mind. A weak mind is like a dandelion, floating aimlessly, being carried away in whichever direction the wind takes it. The dandelion has no control over itself; it is totally at the mercy of the wind. A weak mind will fall prey to many vices.

THOUGHTS

The storms of our lives actually run in our minds. We live in the world of conflicts, wherever we see, inside us, at workplace, at home, everywhere. Conflict creates stress and anxiety. What really matters is not the chaos in our lives, but how we react to it. If we have disturbed minds, even a small thing could agitate us and take us away from our path. The most important lesson is to calm the mind, through which we come out of these conflicts and can look at them as an observer. Only then do we have the power to accept or reject them.

Of course there will be temptations while walking your path. Be aware of the fact that if you want success, you cannot afford to fall prey to such temptations. You already know the time frame to reach your destination. A disciplined and focused approach goes a long way in taking us farther on the journey toward our goal. To be disciplined, we have to take control of the emotions that pull us away from our goal or purpose.

ASKING FOR HELP

We all need help from time to time. There's nothing wrong in asking for help. On the way to our goals, we may need help at some point or the other. It is nature's way of growth. If we look around us, we will find many are helping others get ahead.

Many times we hesitate to ask for help. We fear being rejected or offending the other person. But why be scared to ask? We don't know from where we may get support or inspiration in our lives. Never feel shy or think you don't deserve it. You will be surprised to see how many people are eager and ready to help. But to receive help, we must first ask.

The key is to ask in a way that does not offend anyone and at the same time get the required thing or help needed. I have found the best way is to ask, "Can you please help me?" Once you get the person's attention, then explain your problem. This in my opinion is the most effective, genuine, and straightforward way to ask for help. Hardly anyone gets offended if we are sincere in asking.

If you can offer something in return, that's even better. It may not be the same thing or service in return. Most often a sincere "Thank you" will suffice. Asking for help will also builds up a credible network of people around you. People will want to assist or help you again if they know you genuinely appreciated their help.

INSPIRATIONAL GUIDANCE

Reading books is a very effective way of refueling your energy. Books are the best companions, they say. The best part about inspirational books is that we get unadulterated advice and motivation to go ahead when we feel stuck. Talking to or being with people who have achieved something in life gives a boost to our dreams. The energy and enthusiasm they emit is contagious.

One of the best sources of motivation is reading biographies of successful people. A great biography can give valuable lessons on life and wisdom. There are so many things we can learn from those who have lived their lives successfully. Reading a biography can be very exciting as well, because it is another person's life story. In fact, we can find ideas and ways to practice in our own lives, through the experiences of others. Find one that inspires you the most and read it as often as possible. Keep a good biography handy, maybe at your bedside, so you can read it whenever you are feeling down or depressed.

Another idea is to make a list of people around you who inspire you. Try to meet with them as often as possible, weekly or monthly. Connecting with these achievers and discussing ideas with them will fill you with energy and keep you motivated.

Collect names of people unrelated to your field of passion. This will give you ideas about how people in other areas of work think. More importantly, talking to them will fill your mind with fresh new thoughts and ideas; you may come across a new perspective for a problem or a new outlook toward life itself.

Make another list of people (you don't know directly) who you would like to meet before you die. Keep reading their quotes or blogs, listen to their podcasts, and follow them on social media to keep you charged up.

What inspires others may not be your thing. There may be something else that brings the best out of you. I urge you to find what suits you the most. It may be an inspirational movie or a song or a video or simply dancing to your favorite music.

For some, spending time with children is inspiring. For me, spending time and long walks in the midst of nature or going on long drives works wonders.

REVIEW THE PROGRESS

It is a good practice to review our progress as we go ahead. Ask yourself from time to time, "Where will I be ten years from now if I keep moving the way I am?" If the answer does not take you closer to your chosen goals, think of revising or changing your path.

We can divide our goals into short-term and long-term. Set a timetable for achieving these goals. What do you want to achieve in the next ten years? In the next five years? In the next two years? In the next year? In the next month or week? If you have a solid plan with a timetable, you are more likely to act on it. You should make this plan sacrosanct. Keeping it at a place where you can see it often is a good idea. You can also get it framed and keep it within eyesight. After all, it is your life plan. Isn't it most sacred or important for you to see every day?

The next step is to follow this timetable, unless you want your goals to be mere dreams. Have a ready action plan and then take action. Make a to-do list for your monthly, weekly, and daily goals. That makes the review easy, and tells you whether you are progressing toward your goals. Periodic execution, checking, and revision of goals will give you the motivation and energy to reach your goals. A great success is the ultimate result of smaller successes.

BE THE BEST IN WHATEVER YOU DO

An eagle knows the unlimited freedom of the sky, right from its birth. Similarly, it is our right to experience the boundless joy and freedom of excellence in our life, as humans. We have come on this planet to realize our immense potential and achieve true success. Nothing can hold us back, whether it is a situation, person, thought, feeling, or our circumstances. We are born to shine, excel in all respects.

Everything around us is just perfect, the whole universe, our solar system, the planets, stars, our oceans, atmosphere, rivers, mountains, trees, and animals. So are we, our life, relationships, challenges, situations, circumstances, rewards, etc., just perfect—a miracle. If it is not, that is for a higher purpose.

We must nurture our goals, our vision for life.

Visualize exactly how you feel, see, hear, when you get there, when you experience the fulfillment of your life ambitions and goals, using the best of your imagination. Keep innovating your ways, constantly learning and updating yourself in the process. Constantly look for better ways of doing things or achieving your goals. Keep practicing the talents and improving the finer skills.

Excellence is a not a single event, but a continuous process of improving greatness. Excellence is a habit of doing things in the best possible way. You should always keep in mind that there has to be a better way of achieving something, and always search for it. Nothing is impossible if you have confidence in your capabilities. Your dreams can be limitless, as you are its creator. When you understand this truth and trust your power to achieve them, you can chalk out a plan to accomplish them in real life. Keep building upon your smaller successes.

STEPPING STONES

Most of us fear failure. What we need to understand is that failures can never stop success. In fact, once we learn our lesson from the failures, it leads us to success. Our past failures are actually the groundwork of our future successes. Every time we fail or experience rejection, we get closer to doing it the right way. We just need to keep trying despite the disappointments and adversities. We need to put our failures behind and move forward.

Our failures give us the confidence to move forward with a positive intention. Our longing for success needs to be greater than our fear of failure. We must take the right steps toward our goals. The choice is ours. To become great, to achieve the set goals in life and to walk the purpose, one of the most important ingredients is to be unstoppable. At times you might encounter huge roadblocks on the path to success. The solution is to change your perspective of looking at them and march ahead. You just need to break open the trap of beliefs. Once you are able to achieve that, even the sky is not the limit.

AT A GLANCE

- After taking the first step toward your goal, do not stop.

- To be unstoppable, it is essential to practice discipline and control over the mind.

- What really matters is not the chaos in your life, but how you react to it.

- Excellence is a not a single event, but a continuous process of improving greatness.

CONCLUSION
THE NEXT STEP

Congratulations! You have learned powerful ways to improve your life by reading Key #1, Heal Your Past and Key #2, Live Your Present. Reaching this point is an indication that you have a strong intention to start living a no-regrets life.

You now have a light and healed past, awareness of your true potential, and the wisdom to handle any eventuality and opportunity. Just remember to listen to your inner voice and make the right choices. Be sure, you will soon achieve everything you've always wanted—a stress-free and regret-free life, great relationships, and overall success.

During your journey, remember to contribute to the community, society, mother earth, and the universe.

Remember, Healing, Living, and Planning (HLP) is an ongoing process. Don't hesitate to read the book or a chapter again when you are stuck at any point in your life. The HLP process is not a one-time activity, for hurdles will keep coming your way. We continuously create a past that in turn affects our present and future. Life is full of unforeseen obstacles and circumstances, so keep the KEYS handy and you will never fail. They will help you focus on your ultimate goal.

TAKE HELP, GIVE HELP

Stay connected with people who follow the HLP principle. If you're having trouble in some aspect, seek support from these friends. Also, help others follow the KEYS. One of our responsibilities is to help others find their journey and purpose. So be the KEY in someone else's life and push him or her ahead. Buy another KEYS book or two and gift the book to those who really need it and be a reason for change in their lives.

Give the best to your company. If you are a team leader, boss, director, manager, or CEO of your company, you can take even more advantage of KEYS. If an employee follows the HLP principle, he or she will have a completely healed past, will be living in the present, and planning for the future effectively; making that employee a better performer and a greater asset to your company. KEYS will enhance team work as HLP also deals with forming effective relationships. With KEYS, your employees can give their best to your organization. This in turn will help your organization achieve greater heights.

FORM A KEY CHAIN

Before the launch of this book, I organized a reading at my home. Even though the event was meant to generate criticism for the book in order to improve it, after every chapter the group started discussing the ideas presented and shared their personal stories relating to it. This led to the idea of starting KEYS discussion groups. Reading and understanding the ideas of HLP is important, but discussing it with a group takes it to a greater level. It's a support group enabling you to learn from other people's experiences and mistakes as well. You can motivate and inspire each other. And grow together.

Now, go ahead, live your life to the fullest and enjoy each moment!

DEDICATED TO MY WIFE AND SOUL MATE, ARUNA.

I stand today only because you are by my side

As you held me during life's every tide.

You give me the strength, the energy and force,

The brilliant creative ideas, of which you are the source.

No words can thank enough, for all you did for me,

Your love, unending support, and trust deeper than sea.

I can say now what they say about success is true

'Cause behind my story, there is a woman like you.

ACKNOWLEDGMENTS

This being my first book, I went through all the challenges a first-time author goes through. Moreover, I realized that although I could talk on all the topics in this book for hours together, penning them seemed like a humongous task at times. But there are some wonderful souls who came forward to make this mission a grand success. My deepest gratitude to all of them.

Aruna, my wife, for believing in me more than I believed in myself. She stood behind me like a rock, supporting me in every possible way. She played the roles of worst critic and best advisor.

I am blessed to have a family who was always by my side through thick and thin. I thank my parents for showering their unconditional love and blessings, and for their immense support and faith in my endeavor. I also thank Aruna's parents for their support and blessings.

The idea of this book came when Sanjeev Latkar and I were discussing our favorite topic "life" in his office. He suggested I write a book around this concept, and here it is. Thanks, Sanjeev, for your encouragement and support all through.

My heartfelt gratitude to two wonderful souls, Madhu Sahoo and Meirah Bhastekar, for trusting and showing confidence in me and my book. Since the topic was so close to my heart there was an abundant flow of thoughts and ideas. Putting these together in a constructive way was a task for me. Madhu and Meirah helped me put these together in a very interesting way, using their literary skills.

I wish to sincerely thank my friends Jyotsna Nair, Preeti Singh, Bhavin Shah, Poonam Tandon, Rahul Patel, Reema Pawa, and Jimmy for their valuable feedback on the book that helped me fine-tune it.

Thanks, Parveen Shaikh, for a superbly designed Website and the never-ending support thereafter. I really appreciate your dedication toward work.

I wish to thank Sonia Swaroop Choksi for active support in New Delhi.

There are a few people who were not directly involved with the book, but their contribution to my life's journey and hence the book is priceless. I wish to thank Vaishali and Rakesh Pedram, Priti and Amit Savoor, Pallavi Shinde, Aekta Kapoor, Ramki, Nitin Deshmukh, Puneet Gupta and Suma Varughese. All of you have a very special place in my heart and thanks a million for always being there for me.

This book would be incomplete without mentioning all those who have attended my workshops, talks, seminars, and sessions. Thanks to each and every one of you for believing in me, and for becoming an integral part of my family. Without you, I don't exist.

In addition to all the foregoing, I am filled with gratitude as I humbly prostrate at my Guru's feet, Nityanand Swami of Ganeshpuri. I was always divinely guided and protected throughout. At times I was amazed at how the wisdom just flowed in when I sat to write. This book was only possible because of His infinite love and grace.